THE BLUEPRINT:

A B.S.U. HANDBOOK

By Agyei Tyehimba

DEDICATION

To Malcolm X, one of the 20th Century's most effective Black liberation theorists and critics of white supremacy: His relentless calls for self-determination, self-reliance, self defense and the reaffirmation of Black/African identity helped inspire the formation of the Black Power Movement, Black Student Unions, and Black Studies Departments in the United States.

To Jimmy Garrett, Jerry Varnado and the Black students at San Francisco State University, who started the first Black Student Union in 1966. May we continue to honor your vision and emulate your spirit.

To Black and African-American Studies Departments across the nation: These departments represent the manifestation of Brother Malcolm's call for relevant Black history and analysis. Many of these departments are 40 + years old, and despite constant attacks from white academia, have played a major role in providing an empowering counternarrative of the Black experience and in producing new generations of committed and conscious Black intellectuals. BSUs, working with community activists and intellectuals, fought tirelessly to establish these departments on predominantly white college campuses. May Black Studies faculty and administrators remain true to the original intention and mission of such departments and resist the pressures to become disconnected and careerist like traditional academic disciplines.

To Black Student Union officers: The original founders and pioneers in the 60s and those who served on my executive board, 1988-89; Leslie Copeland, Dina Abrams (Rice), and Samuel Reynolds, and Johnny Polanco, Rachel Hall, and Danielle Stennett, 1989-1990. I also thank and appreciate Tanya Hazelhurst (Dawkins), Karen Mason, Stacey Glover, Aiesha Wilson, Charles "Chuck Wynder, Frank Williams, Kamau M'Bhaso, Ama Tanksley, Moikgantsi Kgama, and so many others. Thank you for your leadership and noble efforts to protect and advance Black interests at Syracuse University.

To current and future BSU officers and general members: May you continue the legacy of your predecessors by challenging oppression, raising political consciousness and creating a safe and productive space for Black students on campus now and in the future. May you also remember the true goal of a liberal arts education for Black people: to acquire and develop the information, ideas, skills, habits and networks that will enable Black students to become leaders and problem-solvers in the community. Certainly, you must financially sustain yourselves, and part of your education should assist in that endeavor. But if you truly believe that you spent all of that time, energy and money in college simply to secure employment within white corporations or agencies, you've missed the point entirely.

"*Those who profess to favor freedom and yet deprecate agitation are men who want crops without plowing up the ground; they want rain without thunder and lightning. They want the ocean without the awful roar of its many waters. This struggle may be a moral one, or it may be a physical one, and it may be both moral and physical, but it must be a struggle. Power concedes nothing without a demand. It never did and it never will. Find out just what any people will quietly submit to and you have found out the exact measure of injustice and wrong which will be imposed upon them, and these will continue till they are resisted with either words or blows, or with both. The limits of tyrants are prescribed by the endurance of those whom they oppress.*"
-Frederick Douglass, 1857

TABLE OF CONTENTS

The BSU Handbook

Foreword

I served as President of my undergraduate Black Student Union for two years (1988-1990) at Syracuse University and President of the Africana Graduate Student Association for one year (1996-1997) while working on my Master's degree in Africana Studies at Cornell University.

These experiences contributed greatly to my own growth as a leader and activist, by helping me to sharpen specific skills like public speaking, editorial writing, negotiating, and conflict mediation, in addition to presiding over meetings, strategic thinking, and leading large campaigns.

My college Black Student Union called the "Student African-American Society" (SAS) was very successful and productive during my undergraduate years. Strong leaders and committed members infused our organization with a sense of purpose, raised political consciousness and organized Black students to empower and advocate for ourselves.

SAS brought accomplished and inspiring Black speakers to campus. These writers, political activists, intellectuals and others became our informal mentors and professors. We KNEW that we were a great people capable of great things and responsible for using our educational privileges in service to our communities. We participated in protests, demonstrations and press conferences to defend Black interests, challenge injustice, and make the campus safer and more empowering for Black students.

I do not exaggerate when I suggest that many powerful and accomplished professionals, activists, intellectuals, educators, artists, and entrepreneurs - who were Syracuse University students in the 80s and 90s - came into their initial sociopolitical consciousness via SAS' influence, whether they admit this or not. BSUs across America exerted a similar influence on innumerable Black students during the 80s and early 90s. During this time, BSUs were highly energetic, visible and politically engaged (as I will address later).

I wrote this book as a practical guide and blueprint primarily for Black Student Unions leaders/executive boards. The specific objective of this book is to provide BSUs around the country with my accumulated knowledge, insight, and experiences, as a former BSU leader on the undergraduate and graduate levels. My hope is that BSUs will use this book to gain clarity and proficiency with specific organizational issues like leadership training, organizing meetings, tactics and strategies for creating campus movements/campaigns, using propaganda, forming alliances and coalitions, making sound leadership decisions, etc.

In a larger sense, this book is a call to action for Black college students in general, to become more politically engaged and to use their formative years in college as a time to develop the leadership skills and strategic thinking so needed in our communities beyond college.

I am not of the opinion that college-educated Black people are the naturally ordained, innate or sole leaders of our community. The criteria as I see it, for effective Black leadership are *consciousness, commitment, sincerity and competence*. By these standards, leadership is not elitist, but inclusive of all strata within our community, regardless of income, education, title, gender, political/religious ideology or social status.

At the same time, Black college students do have access to information and technology which history and prudence suggests they use for our collective empowerment of our people who have not and will not acquire college access. We must also remember that Black college students played pivotal roles in both the Civil Rights and Black Power Movements of the 60s and 70s. Their unbridled idealism, disposable time and energy, coupled with their exposure to alternative ideas/perspectives and freedom from the burdens of career and family obligations, make Black students prime candidates for serious activism.

Finally, there is the realization that while this book (in title and spirit) targets Black college students and BSUs, much of the information here is equally useful and applicable to Black community activists, social justice-oriented nonprofits and Black people who want to become involved in organizing and activism or do so with greater impact.

The burden of leadership and activism does not fall upon black college students alone; all of us are oppressed or negatively affected by white supremacy, corporate exploitation, and government negligence and corruption, therefore all Black people shoulder some responsibility for becoming active agents of resistance and Black empowerment.

You must excuse me then for sincerely hoping and believing that *this book will find its way into the hands and minds of every single BSU in America* in addition to countless Black activists or aspiring activists and organizations in this country and throughout the world.

Introduction

If you listen closely to elected officials, you will hear them repeatedly denounce and dismiss what they call "Special Interests" or "Special Interest groups." Of course, these terms comprise coded language referring to issues or people that are either non-white, non-male, non-privileged, or simply "non-important." Typically, Blacks, Latinos, women, the poor, and many other marginalized people comprise such "special interests."

Fortunately, organizations comprised of committed people form to protect and advance these varied "special interests." Unions for example represent the "special interests" of workers and in doing so are responsible for making the workplace more tolerable and empowering for all of us. Tenant associations fight to protect the "special interests" of people that rent apartments in residential buildings. All renters have such groups to thank for the establishment of rent caps, written leases which clearly specify rental terms, tenant and landlord responsibilities, housing courts, and a list of protective regulations with which so-called "landlords" must comply. In similar fashion Black Student Unions formed in the 60s and 70s to represent the "special interests" of Black students attending thousands of predominately white colleges and universities throughout the nation.

These initial organizations came into being during the tail end of Civil Rights crusades and the birth of Black Power. It is my opinion that too many Black Student Unions today have abandoned the tradition of consciousness-raising, resistance, and Black empowerment they were created to maintain. Political rallies, demonstrations, protests, political education for high school and college students, support for Black Studies Departments, cultural programming and demands to recruit and retain Black faculty and students are now too often replaced with cookouts, fashion shows, parties, and apolitical Hip Hop concerts.

Certainly these events have their place on a college campus, but when such events take place to the exclusion of serious and sustained political activity, by an organization founded specifically to take political positions, we have a serious problem on our hands. Naturally, my critique does not apply to *all* BSUs; some have valiantly continued and expanded on the work of their predecessors. Unfortunately, in an era when some boast of America being "post-racial", political and community-oriented BSUs are exceptions, not the rule.

My critique of contemporary Black Student Unions is informed from the perspectives of being a practitioner and scholar of Black student activism. During the late 80s as an undergraduate student at Syracuse University, I had the honor of being a two-term President of the Student African American Society (SAS). While I was conscious prior to becoming a college student, I came into my own as a leader and organizer because of SAS and its example. Later, as a graduate student at Cornell University, where I was President of the Africana Graduate Student Association, I wrote my Master's thesis about the Black student struggle to create Black Studies Departments on college campuses during the Civil Rights and Black Power Movements. As a doctorate student in African American Studies, I have focused my research around Brother Malcolm X (along with Robert F. Williams) and his pivotal ideological influence on Black student activism during the Black Power Movement.

This incredible journey of activism and scholarship began with my experiences as an undergrad at Syracuse University. SAS was our Black Student Union. This organization represented the issues and interests of all Black undergraduates on campus and did so for about 20 years prior to my arrival in 1986.

Besides providing culturally relevant programming for Black students, conducting political education and developing competent Black leadership, SAS created the African American Studies Department (and later fought to maintain and expand it), was instrumental in the fight to secure a Blue-light system on campus (providing protection for students at night), protested CIA recruitment efforts, challenged Apartheid, protested tuition hikes, advocated for Black community members that worked on campus, and held weekly meetings to raise consciousness among our constituents.

We were privileged to receive mentorship from committed faculty members like Dr. Janis Mayes, Dr. Randolph Hawkins, and Dr. Micere Mugo among others. And I am proud to note that many of the students involved with SAS and its leadership have gone on to do important work in the areas of politics, education, film, philanthropy, community development, religion, music, nonprofits, and countless others.

As indicated earlier, SAS did not begin with my arrival to Syracuse University, but almost 20 years earlier in 1967. Several committed and pioneering Black people grew from these experiences and this period as undergrads at Syracuse University. Among these were St. Clair Bourne, the documentary filmmaker, Vaughn Harper, a university basketball star that later became the famous voice of WBLS' "Quiet Storm" radio show for 30 years, and Suzanne DePasse, (who among other things helped discover the Jackson Five, produced the Motown 25th Anniversary telecast, along with "The Temptations" and "The Jacksons" miniseries).

The very first Black Student Union began a year earlier at San Francisco State University, the same campus where a year-long student strike led to the creation of the nation's first Black Studies Department in 1968. Organized mostly by student and young Civil Rights activist Jim Garrett, the organization essentially placed various Black groups and students under one umbrella (hence "Union") and set out to advocate for Black liberation, solidarity and increased opportunities for Blacks on campus.

Within a couple of years, BSUs sprang up on white college campuses throughout the country. Along with protesting racial injustice and American militarization in Vietnam, the greatest institutional legacy of BSUs was their successful fight for Black Studies Departments. Proactive, political minded and committed Black students (along with community activists, intellectuals and artists) are largely responsible for creating a Black student/intellectual presence on white college campuses, and creating numerous employment and political opportunities for Black professors.

The term "Sankofa" is a Ghanaian concept originating from the Akan people. It means *"It is not a crime to go back and fetch what you have lost."* With this in mind, I issue a Sankofa call to contemporary BSUs who have abandoned serious and sustained political struggle and have become in too many instances, clubs providing entertainment and opportunities to socialize. Your very presence as Black college students is testimony to the struggle and vision of those who came before you. *Let other groups on campus entertain and socialize.* Black Student Unions have a mandate to agitate, organize and politicize. This is especially true since white supremacy is still alive and well and Black Studies Departments around the country face downsizing and questions of their "relevance" from white university officials. We cannot forget the realization that many American citizens of all backgrounds believe America has moved past racial conflict and racism, even while racist White Student Unions appear now, describing slavery as a beneficial institution for Black people and spouting white supremacist and ultra-conservative rhetoric. Now more than ever, Black college students must be politically engaged and highly organized!

I also issue a Sankofa call to Black professors and BSU advisors. Many of you were part of the first BSUs in this country. As seasoned elders in the struggle, you have an obligation to descend from the ivory tower, mentor Black Student Unions and push them to continue the legacy upon which they were built. If we fail in this responsibility, who will be there to protect and advance our "special interests" on American college campuses?

This "Blueprint" is a tool I hope Black Student Unions will use to heed my "Sankofa Call." Within it are the attitudes, information and best practices you can use to make your BSU purposeful and effective. You will notice that most chapters are short, some no longer than 5 pages. My goal is not to write a rigorous scholarly text or award-winning prose, but a concise, precise leadership/activism manual. Based on my research this is the first book of its kind written specifically for Black Student Unions. My hope is that other Black organizations will also see this book as a tool they can use for practical information, as many of the ideas discussed here are universal. My goal here has absolutely nothing to do with style, but everything to do with substance.

The Purpose of a BSU

We must begin at the beginning. Before we discuss strategies, tactics, press conferences and protests, we must be absolutely and unequivocally clear on our role. What is the purpose of a Black Student Union? Who do we serve, and how do we serve them? How is the BSUs role and purpose separate and distinct from those of other campus organizations?

If we were to view the constitutions of several contemporary BSUs we would find several stated interpretations of their purpose or objectives. I've provided some sample BSU purpose statements (taken from actual BSU Constitutions) A Midwestern BSU states as its purpose:

To promote the recognition and involvement of African American students with the intention of creating a strong voice on campus and to make an impact on the decisions regarding students of the University Community. Encourage academic achievement and personal development in leadership, time management, organizational and communication skills among the membership. Promote both academic and extracurricular programs to enhance and increase knowledge and appreciation of cultural diversity.

A BSU located at a Mid-Atlantic university states:

The purpose of the Black Student Union shall be education, group unity, business networking, entrepreneurial encouragement, and community development.

A Western BSU asserts:

1) Access, retention, and yield programming to inspire, to enlighten, to build unity, to challenge, and to perpetuate the ideologies of the BLACK STUDENT UNION.

2) To support the efforts of those organizations which perpetuate the ideologies of the BLACK STUDENT UNION.

3) To assist in providing an environment that is conducive to academic excellence amongst the African American student population.

A Southern BSU maintains:

> *Our purpose is to facilitate cultural awareness and dialogues in social responsibility. In addition to coordinating creative and relevant programs and educating the campus about the rich diversity of black and African American culture we will examine and address issues that impact people of African descent both locally and globally. Participate in community service that will enhance our community and uplift the human condition.*

Lastly, an Ivy League BSU defines its purpose in the following way:

> *The purpose of BSU shall be to operate as a focal point for Black cultural, political and social activities on the campus. Through student input, BSU will strive to foster cooperation and unity between individuals who descend from the African Diaspora and those interested in learning about Black culture.*

You will notice variations among how these BSUs throughout America define their purpose. Interestingly, these samples are representative of the trends we see around the country. In general, we can sort these organizations into three general categories: 1. Those with a strong middle class focus on academic and career preparation 2. Those seeking to promote cultural awareness and consciousness 3. BSUs focusing on socio-political engagement and programming.

As I mentioned in the introduction to this book, the student architects of the first Black Student Unions were politically conscious people strongly concerned with Black empowerment, community service, liberation, and social justice. They were also concerned with securing academic resources for their members ensuring that universities hired Black professors to teach Black history, politics, and other disciplines, and to coordinate Black solidarity and cooperation. The original BSUs fought against elitist tendencies by opening their meetings to members of the larger Black community surrounding the campus. They established chapters in high schools and coordinated tutoring programs for students in local public schools. They fought to provide cultural reaffirmation.

It is my opinion that contemporary BSUs should combine elements of all three categories I previously discussed. Comprehensively speaking, the role of a Black Student Union is to advocate for Black students, increase their opportunities for self-development and collective empowerment, develop an appreciation for African and Black identity and culture, challenge unjust university policies, acts and ideas that oppress and restrict Black students, and work to cultivate a spirit and practice of Black solidarity on campus and beyond.

To their credit, many BSUs do embody some of these elements, but far too many spend precious time, energy and student fee funding hosting elaborate social events that fulfill little to none of the objectives I just outlined. In the spirit of building and maintaining morale for group members, Black Student Unions should set time aside to sponsor events allowing members to mix, mingle and have fun. Given that numerous other campus organizations exist specifically for socializing, BSUs have a mandate to host such events sparingly.

A separate but related issue is having a clear understanding of *who* Black Student Unions, or African American Societies serve. There is an increasing tendency among such groups to see themselves as serving "people of color," or "students" on campus. As is self-evident in the very names of these organizations, the people served and represented by BSUs are Black or African American, students. "People of color" denotes a much wider demographic including Latinos, Asians, and Native Americans, all of whom have existing campus organizations devoted to representing them. Black Student Unions were created on the principle of self-determination; BSUs have a mandate to empower, educate and advocate for Black students, not the entire campus or the entire pantheon of melanated students. This does not mean that BSUs cannot or should not work with other populations. It means that our focus was, is, and should continue to be **ourselves!**

Now that we have a clear understanding of what our purpose is, we can participate in activities/projects that fulfill that purpose and meet our objectives. This helps to keep the organization consistent, and helps guide our decisions; This is important to BSU leaders, as you should make all decisions from the standpoint of how such decisions or choices align with your organizational objectives.

Leadership Training

All effective organizations require leadership and contrary to the popular saying, leaders are **not** born, they are made. Most seasoned leaders in any field acquire their skills and wisdom through a combination of experience and training. Because we do not know each officer's level of leadership experience, and cannot rely on new officers to have the skills needed to run our organizations, we must take the initiative and develop leadership training for them. In my experience and from what I've observed, many BSUs do not have a structured and effective process for training/preparing newly-elected officers.

What then, is the importance of leadership training? This might seem self-explanatory, but it deserves some clarity. *Leadership training is not a useless formality or something we do impulsively.*

Leadership training is a necessity, not an option, and not something we can take lightly or trivialize. If you choose to do so, you do so at your own risk! Leadership training should equip newly elected officers with the skills, knowledge, habits and contact people they need to effectively execute their responsibilities and provide capable service/representation to the organization. It's safe to say that we can make a direct correlation between an organization's level of leadership training and its overall effectiveness. Sure, some highly motivated and exceptional officers will do their own independent research in this area or may come with the basic skills needed. But again, we cannot afford to rely on such occurrences.

You might ask, "What components do we include in our leadership training? The answer is that the duties and requirements of leading your organization and your organizational objectives shape your leadership training. I must insist that you approach this matter strategically, not in an arbitrary manner.

Drawing from the objectives we outlined for BSUs, it would appear that all newly-elected officers at minimum should:

- ✓ Be introduced to university staff and fellow student leaders they'll have to work with during their tenure as BSU officers. For example, the BSU Treasurer should meet and know the treasurer or comptroller of the entire student body. Officers should also meet other Black student leaders on campus or leaders of organizations the BSU typically works closely with.

✓ Learn how to complete and submit important paperwork such as requisitions to purchase supplies, or the payroll forms needed to ensure that contracted performers, vendors or speakers get paid on time.

✓ Know how to accurately keep and securely store the BSU's financial records

✓ Know how to organize and conduct press conferences and write press releases

✓ Be familiar with how to co-sponsor events with other campus organizations

✓ Know how/where to access and contribute to the organization's archives (fliers, newspaper articles, photographs, audio and/or video recorded events, etc.)

✓ Be familiar with their university's organization chart, or hierarchy of leadership (Who runs/does what for the university, who to target in case of dispute)

✓ Know how to program events (search for and secure speakers, performers and vendors, arrange for food and refreshments, make sure contracted people are paid on time, etc.)

✓ Be thoroughly familiar with the BSU Constitution, By-laws and special procedures

✓ Know how to arrange/conduct meetings (reserve rooms, arrange for audio/visual equipment, set meeting agendas, etc.

✓ Make copies, purchase office equipment and other supplies

✓ Structure and conduct rallies, protests and demonstrations

✓ Be able to create and maintain a database of members and use email or social media to disseminate information to them

✓ Be familiar with major benchmarks or highlights in the BSU's history

✓ Be prepared to speak effectively to groups

✓ Be able to write effectively, particularly with respect to editorials and press releases

✓ Be able to use computer software to create fliers, brochures and other promotional items

BSU leaders ultimately must determine the content and scope of their leadership training content and process, taking into account the duties of new officers, campus dynamics and intended outcomes. I have simply provided a brief outline of why such training is important, and certain things it should include.

Additional things to consider

- Academic years range from 91/2 to 10 months. This means that BSU elections should occur long before the end of the school year so incoming officers have enough time to train before summer break. I would suggest holding BSU elections in December prior to Winter/Christmas break. New officers would not begin officially until the upcoming fall semester, but would receive leadership training from January of the New Year until April, prior to final exams.

- BSUs can ensure a highly competent team of new officers *before* election time. Current leaders can record video workshops that cover much of the content in your leadership training program. Using certain software, any BSU member can go through the leadership training program by logging in, completing the workshops at their own pace, and even taking a quiz at the conclusion of each unit. Upon completion, people can print out a certificate proving that he or she completed training in a satisfactory manner. You can require all candidates for BSU offices to produce this certificate, or give newly-elected officers a deadline by which they complete this training.

- Different leadership positions have different duties and require different skill sets. Therefore leadership training for the President might differ from that of a Treasurer or Vice President. Your Executive Board will need to identify which things all officers should know versus the things that are specific to certain positions. However I would recommend that the President know how to execute the duties of all positions.

- As this book is written specifically for BSUs, consider using it as part of your leadership training.

Meetings

All Black Student Unions, African-American Societies or the like, hold regular meetings for members. I want to spend some time discussing why we have these meetings, what should be accomplished at these meetings, how to run these meetings in an organized fashion, and how to get more members out to these meetings.

Purpose of General Meetings

General meetings are those held for all BSU constituents/members. We hold these meetings to:

- Provide members with information concerning upcoming events, updates, interesting opportunities, etc.

- Discuss particular issues of importance to the general body

- Receive suggestions and feedback from the general body

- Develop and maintain morale

- Conduct political education for members

- Solicit volunteers for organizational projects

- Address questions or concerns members might have

- Coordinate BSU projects, initiatives, campaigns

- Provide opportunities for members to get involved

General Guidelines

- To maintain consistency, most BSUs hold weekly meetings. If possible, these meetings should occur in the same room, same day of the week and same time every week

- In consideration of students' study and personal schedule, it is preferable to limit meetings to one hour in length

- Meetings should begin promptly and end promptly regardless of how many people are present (unless your constitution calls for a certain number of people or quorum in order to conduct business).

- A secretary should be present at every meeting to take minutes. The secretary should also post abbreviated minutes online so members that have missed meetings can stay informed. This also creates a backup copy of all minutes.

- All meetings should have an agenda which is disseminated to members or written/projected for members to see. The agenda serves to prevent the meeting facilitator from forgetting to discuss something, and also tells the general body what they will discuss or accomplish. Typical meeting agendas include a welcome, review of minutes from the last meeting, old business, new business and a closing. To ensure that meetings progress in a timely manner, you can designate a specific amount of time to each agenda item.

- *BSU meetings should never be boring!* While the President usually chairs meetings, other officers should have roles to play as well. No one person should do all of the talking. Meetings should cover material that is relevant and engaging. Officers should take great care to have members participate and give input. Members should be encouraged to debate issues, come up with ideas and ask questions. Also, meetings should sometimes involve viewing video clips, discussing news, or listening to songs that pertain to the topic at hand. In short, your members should *enjoy* BSU meetings, and want to invite other Black students to attend in the future.

- General meetings provide an excellent opportunity to enlist the aid of the general body. You should always have flyers announcing upcoming events available for members in attendance to post or distribute in their dorms.

- You should take time at every general meeting to identify people attending for the first time. Have them complete a form with their phone number, email address, skills and other relevant information; Later the secretary will enter this information into the BSU database. This database is important, as it provides the means for contacting members to inform them of events, emergency meetings, meeting cancellations, or to enlist their help to complete certain tasks.

- Every campus student organization derives its budget from student-fee money paid by every undergraduate on campus. Universities typically insist that since every student contributes to this fee, campus organizations must be open to and benefit ALL students at the university. This stipulation however does not give non-members (white students) the right to attend BSU meetings. Black Student Unions must have the space to discuss topics and handle business without distractions, diversions, or the need to respond to outsider's interests and concerns. You are therefore within your right to politely inform white students that anyone can attend your events, but only recognized constituents (Black students) can attend general meetings. This will prove especially important when your organization becomes involved in protests or other controversial actions requiring you to discuss ideas with privacy and discretion.

- Because students might not have eaten prior to your meetings it might be a good idea to provide simple refreshments like juice, water, cheese, crackers or fruit if your budget allows you to. The proper BSU official will arrange this with the university's dining services department. Keep in mind that expenditures for these things must be low.

Executive Board Meetings

"E-Board" Meetings as they are sometimes called, provide opportunities for BSU officers to meet and discuss things from a leadership point of view. You want to develop an agenda for your upcoming general meeting, tie up any loose ends regarding upcoming events and coordinate any new initiatives or updates you plan on sharing with BSU members. The President uses this time to "spot check" and make sure every officer has completed their designated tasks, or understands what they need to do. The bulk of these meetings consist of following up on previous ideas, checking items off the list, and discussing what remains to be done. Because these meetings tend to be heavy on dates and information, the secretary should be present to take minutes.

Each officer should give a brief verbal report at this meeting, outlining what they have accomplished, unfinished business, and concerns they have. When officers choose or are assigned tasks, timetables must be established. That is, you all must agree on a specific date by which a said task will be completed.

Remember, meetings serve very specific and important functions. Well planned, productive, informative and inclusive meetings are the building blocks of a powerful and effective organization.

Programming

By programming, I refer to all the organizational events and activities planned and implemented by the BSU. Again, these activities are not created randomly. All BSU programming in some way embodies or promotes BSU objectives and the BSU image. Here we see the importance of having a clearly defined vision in the beginning; all other decisions and activities stem from this vision.

This means that BSU officers should not simply repeat the same type of events the organization has traditionally done. Of course, some events have very important meaning for the organization and play an important role in maintaining continuity.

When an event or activity is proposed, BSU officers should be able to explain: 1) how the event advances or embodies the objectives articulated in its Constitution 2) How the event is beneficial or detrimental to the BSUs image or prestige, etc. 3) The residual benefits of hosting the event or activity.

Residual benefits of hosting an event might include raising the morale and spirits of your group members, attracting positive media attention, recruiting new members, attracting the attention and support of Black people in the local community, creating Black solidarity symbolically or in practice, and increasing awareness of an important issue. I will mention now a few typical examples or BSU programming to provide some context to our discussion.

Public Speakers

Charismatic or highly informed and accomplished public speakers constitute a tried and true type of BSU event. Such individuals inspire, inform, bring prestige (and media coverage) to your organization, and possibly much-needed support to a BSU campaign or issue.

But I would caution against bringing a speaker simply because he/she is a celebrity or simply because he/she is Black. Each and every speaker you invite to campus MUST REPRESENT

ISSUES AND INTERESTS YOUR BSU SUPPORTS. At the very least, your speaker should not go *against* BSU ideas or issues and should present information that positively advances your organizational agenda and your constituents. I cannot emphasize this enough.

Let's say your BSU is fighting for the right to exclude white students from your general meetings. You've advocated this right for months via protests, rallies, and a petition to the University President. Your BSU's position on this issue generates controversy as some perceive this to mean you are separatist or "reverse-racist."

You invite a popular and politically conscious entertainer to speak on campus assuming that they support your position, but fail to clarify that before contracting the speaker. That entertainer shows up on campus, attracts thousands of students and excellent media coverage. BSU officers believe they've hit the jackpot! Then during the Q&A session, a white student leader of a rival organization asks the speaker to comment on the issue of BSU meetings being all-Black. The entertainer to whom you've paid $5000 forcefully explains that he does not agree with the policy; in his opinion, whites should be able to attend your meetings, because this helps combat racial division and ignorance.

Much to your embarrassment, a speaker you've paid to speak on behalf of your organization, has in 30 seconds, undermined an issue you've addressed for several months! I personally witnessed a popular Hip Hop artist do this to a BSU in 1990. The BSU engaged in a fight for self-determination, insisting that they had the right to prohibit white students from attending their general meetings. When asked about this, the rap artist strongly denounced the group's position. Needless to say, the damage he did to the BSU and its struggle around this issue was incalculable.

The speakers you select must push your agenda forward, not sabotage it. If you want them to endorse your position on an issue, you must confirm this with them before they speak. Of course you can prevent such error simply by understanding every speaker's politics prior to booking them.

The BSUs I led, both at Syracuse University and Cornell University, were progressive-minded, nationalist-oriented, and pushing for Black self-determination and empowerment. We were not afraid to take controversial positions if we believed in them. The speakers we brought to campus reflected this: Minister Louis Farrakhan, Kama Ture, Susan Taylor, Naim Akbar, Khallid Muhammad, Dr. Betty Shabazz, Gil Noble, Sista Souljah, and Nikki Giovanni, among others.

As a result of our programming with respect to speakers, our constituents received a first-class education and level of Black consciousness that academic classes couldn't provide. Such speakers energized us to fearlessly challenge racist forces on and off campus and helped us to be successful in doing so.

Cookouts

BSUs often host year-ending cookouts. These events are obviously recreational in nature and play a very important role in bringing our constituents together and enjoying good food and music. Students who have faced an entire year of exams, labs, stressful papers, protests and press conferences, rightly look forward to some fun leisure time.

However cookouts can become more than just socializing events simply by holding them at the beginning of the school year. September usually boasts mild temperatures and sunny skies conducive to cookouts.

Furthermore, programming an activity like this in September gives your BSU the added advantage of welcoming/meeting new students, introducing them to the BSU, and recruiting them. I would suggest booking a DJ from the local community, inviting students from the neighboring community and 4-year colleges, and having food that appeals to non-carnivores as well.

If African American, Caribbean and African restaurants exist in the local community, this is a good time to involve them. You can arrange for them to cater certain dishes and bring cards promoting their business. This makes your cookout menu far more diverse, puts money in the pockets of local Black businesses, and encourages new students to come off campus and support these businesses. This by the way helps to build relationships with the local community which will certainly prove crucial later.

You can have BSU officers at information tables getting students' information, and distributing BSU event flyers and organizational buttons/cards as well. The President can make brief introductory and event-ending remarks introducing his/her executive board, informing the crowd of meeting times, and thanking everyone for attending.

Parties and Social Events

Unless your BSU is celebrating a political victory, or attempting to develop morale, I personally find it difficult to justify why this organization should sponsor traditional parties on campus. First of all, Black fraternities and sororities already provide such functions. Second, it is difficult to explain how parties relate to anything in the BSU's constitutional objectives.

Of course, with some creativity, these rules can bend. Creating a poetry cafe complete with live music puts a cultural spin on a traditional party concept. I apply the same logic to fashion shows, formal balls, or date "auctions." Quite frankly, purely social events like this demonstrate a BSU that is disconnected from or ambivalent about its true role on campus.

BSUs should always strive to raise consciousness, challenge Black oppression, and create positive solidarity and support for Black students. As a reminder, all programming you do should accomplish some or all of these objectives. Have you ever seen an outfit that looked good on someone else, but you would not wear it? This is the case with a BSU. Some seemingly good programming ideas are great for other campus organizations, but not so for a BSU.

A fraternity fashion show for example, makes sense. But what is the purpose of a BSU fashion show? How does this event push your organization's agenda? How does it complement your objectives? This is especially true if your fashion show highlights typical American or European styles of fashion. If the fashion show however, highlights African fashions from different nations or features clothing made by local Black designers, the BSU exposes Black students to traditional African culture or brings attention (and hopefully, money) to unrecognized Black designers right in the local community. What if instead of doing a talent show, your BSU organized a telethon featuring Black campus and community talent and took financial pledges from callers to raise money to provide scholarships for needy Black high school students, or fresh-water wells for an African village?

So your challenge is to provide programming that meets your organizational objectives, and to do so in ways that are both creative and engaging.

Propaganda

"Propaganda" is a politically loaded term that we usually think of in negative ways. Yet any effective campus organization or any type of political organization should accurately understand propaganda and be able to use it effectively.

According to Wikipedia, Propaganda is a *"form of communication that is aimed towards influencing the attitude of the community toward some cause or position by presenting only one side of an argument. Propaganda is usually repeated and dispersed over a wide variety of media in order to create the chosen result in audience."* The online reference site Dictionary.com defines propaganda as:

"Attitudes, information, ideas, or rumors which are deliberately spread widely to help or harm a person group, movement, institution, nation, etc."

Propaganda has been used both to justify Ku Klux Klan brutality toward Black people, and to urge the public to stop smoking or driving while drunk. It was used to depict Black people as being unintelligent, naturally violent, and incorrigible. The Black Panthers used it to depict cops in urban areas as "pigs": unnecessarily violent and repressive forces that occupied Black communities. More famously, propaganda is used by the U.S. government to depict certain people as "terrorists" and others as "patriots."

The key to understanding propaganda is that it uses selective language and symbols to steer the public toward thinking and acting in a particular way. It can be used for positive or negative outcomes, and is all around us. Perhaps the most popular and omnipresent forms of propaganda are television commercials, all of which use an array of information (or misinformation), music, and images to persuade us to purchase a particular brand of beer, automobile, cell phone, toothpaste, cereal or any number of products.

BSUs want members to attend meetings, participate in protests, join committees, and attend events. BSUs involved in a campus campaign or movement want faculty, students, and community members to support or be sympathetic to their cause. BSUs seek to recruit new active members or to defend what the larger campus might view a controversial position. Regarding all of these issues and more well-executed propaganda is an investment that can pay high dividends. BSUs must actively and effectively use propaganda; there is no way around this fact. How is this done?

1. Begin with the specific idea or action you want to promote
2. Identify the specific audience you're targeting
3. Identify powerful words or images that represent the idea or action you're promoting
4. Identify values or ideas that audience values, and needs or desires they have
5. Find creative ways using the language and symbols you've identified to persuade your audience to adopt the action or value you're promoting.

In 1943 psychologist Abraham Maslow wrote a paper entitled "A Theory of Human Motivation," which suggested that human beings are motivated to meet certain needs. Most television commercials and various forms of advertisement still draw from Maslow's theory. He categorized human needs into lower and higher levels, and argued that as a person meets lower or more basic needs, they grow to meet higher or more advanced needs. Maslow represented this "Hierarchy of Needs" with a five-tier pyramid. The most basic needs (food, clothing, shelter, etc) comprised the bottom tier. The next tier was safety, then love/belonging, esteem, and the final and top of the pyramid represented what he called "self-actualization. This final and highest level of needs included things like morality, problem-solving, creativity and so on.

Your propaganda will be powerful and effective if you tailor it to address these human needs. In other words, your propaganda pitch should connect and appeal to your audience's needs. Students have a need to feel protected (from tuition increases, racial attack), to belong, to meet basic biological needs, to feel a sense of achievement and to be personally fulfilled.

BSUs should use propaganda via political cartoons, radio shows, articles, slogans, mottos, and demonstrations whenever possible. I would even suggest that BSU members be encouraged to become DJs for campus/community radio stations or start their own weekly SAS internet radio show via blogtalkradio for example. This radio show should address issues the BSU raises, drum up support for the BSU, explain/defend SAS policies/positions, rebroadcast BSU speakers, and feature interviews with progressive-minded Black faculty, community leaders, and BSU speakers.

Use images and words to show how attending your meetings, becoming active in the BSU, attending an event, or participating in your demonstration meets these needs, and your propaganda will prove highly effective.

Know Your Terrain

BSU officers cannot afford to exist on a campus or in a city they know nothing about. Such isolation leads to political weakness. Yet it's surprising how little some student leaders actually know about their college or city wherein that college is located.

Believe me; having such knowledge greatly enhances the power and influence of your BSU in ways you cannot imagine.

Things to know about your college/university

- Who the President is, what his/her politics are, and his/her background

- Board of Trustees members. This board is the true power at any university. Its members are typically wealthy, educated, and considered experts in one field or another. The Board hires or fires the University's President, and is responsible for influencing university policies and raising money for the university. It's also helpful to know when and where they physically meet.

- Popular hangouts or places where students congregate. These are excellent places to distribute flyers or hold rallies and demonstrations

- A general history of the university, especially where Black people are concerned.

- Outspoken and politically conscious professors. They often make excellent mentors/advisors and will often support your BSU during protests and movements. Some of them sit in on university meetings and can offer very privileged information. It also doesn't hurt to be cool with sympathetic members of your college student government.

- Black organizations and non-Black organizations that are socially conscious. BSU presidents should establish relationships with such organizations and their leadership. These relationships will promote solidarity and often yield co-sponsorships for your events in addition to support for your causes.

Things to know about the city/larger community

- Stores that sell products used by your constituents

- Community centers, Barber/Beauty shops, Black churches, restaurants, businesses and Black organizations. These are the hubs of news and political/social activity in Black communities. This is where you'll meet, work with, and form relationships with local Black folk. It is imperative that the Black community know you and be familiar with your BSU. You should always invite community members and leaders to your events and attend theirs. People born and raised in the city where you attend college will be able to share valuable information and resources with you. Often, arrogant Black students act in condescending ways toward Black community residents. BSUs should do everything in their power to break this cycle of ignorance and arrogance. They are Black people just like yourself living in communities similar to your own.

- Popular hangouts or places where Black residents congregate

- Local radio stations, television stations, and newspaper headquarters (especially Black ones if they exist). Developing relationships with the media always comes in handy later. See if you can speak with Black newspaper editors to have a regular column which provides a BSU perspective on life in the city.

Alliances

Campus and community politics involve several powerful institutions and dynamics. This combination often overwhelms BSUs or other Black organizations. What does one do when they're outnumbered by powerful and organized foes? Naturally, you get like-minded people and groups to protect you and support your cause. Street gangs understand this when they merge with other gangs. Nations understand this when they form treaty agreements and partner up in wartime. BSUs must understand this concept as well.

BSUs have organizational opponents and organizational allies on campus. Racist white groups that see Blacks as inferior charity cases that only make progress in life due to playing the "race card" are opposing forces; Groups that deem BSUs reverse racists for advocating Black solidarity and self-determination are opposing forces; Faculty members that mock or attempt to dismiss African civilization or ingenuity are opposing forces. These groups will likely never support your BSU and will possibly make moves to sabotage or mischaracterize your organization and the Black students/issues you represent.

As the forces of racism and white American entitlement continue to organize and push their agenda without consequence, people and groups representing such beliefs will become more bold and assertive.

At Towson University in Maryland for example, a "White Student Union" formed in 2012. Although the university refuses to recognize the WSU as an official campus organization, this racist group went on to patrol the campus at night to protect white students from "Black predators," and to defend slavery as being beneficial to Black people. Interestingly, these types of organizations cite their purpose as the reclamation and promotion of white heritage, despite the fact that most whites attending white universities comprise 60-70% of the campus population. Clearly, elements like these are opponents to groups like a BSU. Regardless of your own personal disposition on whites, please understand that as men in America are conditioned to feel themselves superior to women, so too are whites conditioned with respect to Black people.

Fortunately your organization has plenty of potential allies on campus; among these are progressive-minded faculty members and other student groups. You might also find strong allies in:

1. Black fraternities and sororities,
2. Groups representing Caribbean, African, or Latino students
3. Black graduate student organizations
4. Black professional groups (Black law Association and the National Society of Black Engineers, for example)
5. Campus chapters of national social justice organizations (i.e. NAACP)
6. White liberal or radical student organizations that protest war, pollution, or imperialism

Alliances don't need to be permanent. You can work with other groups around a particular project or cause, without being in any mandatory and ongoing relationship with them.

Guidelines for Alliances

- Alliances work best when all groups share an equilibrium of power. If one or more groups wield significantly more power than the others, they can exert disproportionate influence on the alliance. This can cause problems later on

- Many alliances develop in response to a crisis or conflict. There's nothing wrong with this. However you can also be proactive and develop alliances around common issues and interests prior to any conflict. Proactive formation of alliances better helps you to arrange the resources and infrastructure necessary to prevent some conflicts and to better respond when conflicts arise

- Ideally, an alliance should be a mutually beneficial and collaborative experience; all groups involved should benefit in some way from the alliance. Alliance members should share benefits and risks

- The groups or people you choose to align with don't necessarily need to agree perfectly with all BSU policies or beliefs. However, their views and values should complement those of your Black Student Union and you should not disagree on major issues. How will you work together if you do?

- Your alliance should form around specific issues all groups generally agree on and value.

- Expectations should be clearly explained to all members.

- At the same time, these are independent organizations with their own constituents, schedule of meetings, and events to coordinate. Therefore, alliance activities and meetings should not preclude groups from tending to their own organizational business

- It is perfectly acceptable for one group to take the lead on an issue, but this should be explained in advance and every group should know what role they play in a particular campaign

- Alliance members should appear together at press conferences, rallies and demonstrations to demonstrate solidarity

- Community alliances usually are more formal and permanent than collegiate alliances. They meet regularly and tend to be more lasting. College alliances, given graduations and the constant flux of students, are sometimes more temporary and less formal. You can choose whatever structure fits your needs and circumstances. Sometimes an alliance might be a simple understanding that certain groups will unify around certain common issues like proposed tuition increases or worker's rights. These alliances might agree in principle to support member organization's rallies or protests, or to help disseminate fliers There may be no need for alliances to have regular meetings or any formal agreement. The key point here is for BSU to develop relationships with other groups that share issues and interests, using such alliances to boost their strength and effectiveness by sharing resources and tasks.

How and in what capacity this occurs, are decisions you'll have to make

Utilizing Media

Television, radio, newspaper and Internet media exist to inform, entertain and persuade the public. Since these mediums do exist, and tend to exert great influence on public perception, it is important that BSUs utilize the media effectively. These news mediums will use your protests, rallies and events to provide make their broadcasts exciting and engaging for their audiences. You must use the media to promote the issues and interests of your organization.

In order to utilize the media, you must present them with information they deem "newsworthy." It is a highly subjective term, because only news stations determine what exactly the criteria are and only they decide who meets it. According to CyberCollege.com, a news medium considers approximately 6 things when determining if a story is newsworthy:

1. Timeliness: Mediums are most interested in current events and events or issues that are occurring now

2. The number of people involved or affected

3. Proximity: Stories that occur close to a news medium (city or state) are more appealing than stories that take place far away

4. Prominence: For better or worse, news mediums give great priority to stories concerning famous or "important" people.

5. Human Interest: Human interest stories are designed to evoke emotion and inspire the audience. Referred to as "soft news," this might include stories of children reunited with parents after a natural catastrophe, a generous restaurant owner who provides free food to homeless people, or a person with one leg that runs in a marathon to raise money for people like themselves.

6. Shock Value: Stories involving odd people and unusual circumstances or that feature sensational or scandalous issues are often appealing to news mediums

7. Tragedy: For some reason, the public is often interested in stories that involve tremendous suffering, murder or other types of tragedy.

While all news mediums employ these general criteria of newsworthiness, Different mediums target different senses and therefore favor different formats. It's important to know this so that you appropriately customize your information to each medium and increase your chances of having your story featured.

Radio broadcasting for example, is an auditory business. The radio audience can't see images. The clothing you wear to the studio is therefore not as important as your ability to speak clearly, explain your issue and "paint pictures with your words." Pre-recorded clips of rally speeches, informative interviews, and powerful quotes matter on radio.

Television and the Internet use multimedia including pictures, sound/music, and video. In these mediums your image is more important since you will be seen during interviews and possibly judged based on your appearance. When targeting television news, you want to appeal to the visual aspect. Demonstrations, with their large crowds, loud chants, colorful signs/banners, and possible confrontations with authority figures, are hand-made for television broadcasts.

Print media like newspapers involve powerful images and text. Reporters are likely to cover a story that provides them with strong quotes from credible sources, a concise explanation of the issues involved, and expressive pictures that capture the story.

But how do you inform the media of your issue in a way that interests them in reporting your story? The standard way to do this is by writing a press release.

A press release is a one page document that provides media agencies the Who, What, Where, When and Why of a story along with a person to contact for further information. Releases typically inform media of upcoming events, news stories or important issues your BSU wants to address. You write a press release hoping to have a reporter and/or camera crew come out and cover your event. Alternatively, a reporter might call the contact person listed to do an interview. In any event, a well-written press release is a ticket to securing press coverage and thereby informing the general public about your activities.

General things to consider

1. Always print your press release on official BSU letterhead

2. Make sure press release is addressed/directed to a specific editor or reporter, not "To whom it may concern."

3. Start with a strong headline.

4. Make your point clear in the first paragraph.

5. If possible, quantify data. How many people do you expect to attend? What percentage tuition increase is the university proposing? How many Black students were forced to stop their studies due to financial reasons? This is not an editorial. Use accurate numbers to dramatize your issue/event

6. Make sure it contains NO ERRORS. Some editors are finicky and might disregard your press release for even simple grammatical errors. Use your computer to proofread, and then have someone reliable to proofread it several times before sending it out.

7. Always use relevant quotes from reliable sources (professors, university administrators, community leaders, the BSU president, etc.). This gives your story credibility

8. Always include contact information for your organization's designated media person (usually the president). This includes name, phone number, email address, and the person's title.

9. Try not to exceed one page.

10. Leave a few internet links pertaining to your issue or event, especially those generated by your organization.

Format for a press release

PrWeb.com provides an excellent press release format:

1. *Headline:* Write a headline that is short and simple. It should not be longer than 170 characters and the primary keyword for the release should be included.

2. *Summary Paragraph:* The first paragraph should briefly illustrate what the main point of the release is, including why the information provided is relevant and newsworthy. It should be italicized.

3. *Location & Date Line*: Beneath the summary, begin the opening paragraph of the release with the city and state where the business is located, (the name of the news release distribution service in parentheses), and the date the news release is being made public using the month, day, and year format.

4. *Body*: The body of your news release should start on the same line as the location/date and be separated from it by a dash (–) with one blank space on either side. The body typically consists of two or three paragraphs that are single-spaced and separated with

one blank line in between. Each paragraph should be focused on a single idea and have only a few sentences.

5. *Company Information:* This section should be a standard paragraph that contains a short, factual overview of the business or organization. The same company information statement can be used in each news release that you publish.

6. *Contact Details:* Include information about how readers can contact the appropriate person for additional information. This section should include the name of the appropriate person along with his or her telephone number; email address; and the URL for your organization's website.

Press Conferences

Sometimes you'll send a press release to get reporters to cover an event you're sponsoring. There are also times when your BSU will choose to hold a press conference. Generally, you'll hold a press conference for any number of reasons:

1. To get publicity for your views, events and accomplishments

2. To inform the campus or larger community about your movement

3. To counter negative and inaccurate news concerning your organization

4. To send a message to an individual or organization concerning your demands or grievances

5. To demonstrate the strength and power of your organization

It's important to remember that this is a public relations event. You will be judged by how you perform at this conference. Therefore, you must strategically decide what information is presented, how it's presented, and who presents it.

Your conference should appoint a moderator who will open and close the conference, introduce speakers, and control the flow of the event. You should also designate one or two informed speakers who will give brief statements to the press. Your president – as spokesperson of the BSU - should do the bulk of the speaking and be prepared to concisely and intelligently answer questions from the press.

To prevent redundant statements and boring lapses of time, the moderator should limit questions and the conference itself to a designated time. Also, because you must control every element of how your organization is perceived by the media and your audience, your appointed moderator should have and wisely exercise the authority to determine what questions your spokesperson answers and when the conference concludes. When possible, the BSU president can act as spokesperson and moderator of the press conference.

To insure that you disseminate your message in its entirety, you might want to prepare a one-page information sheet that addresses what you believe to be the most important issues, and give copies of this sheet to all reporters in attendance.

By using these methods and truly understanding how to utilize the media, you can increase the public's awareness of your issue, gain much-needed support, and guard/advance your organizational interests.

BUILDING MORALE

Merriam-Webster dictionary defines morale as *"The common spirit existing in the members of a group and inspiring enthusiasm, devotion, and strong regard for the honor of the group."* Simply put, morale is the glue that holds an organization together and the fuel that propels it forward. An organization can be clear on its purpose, have excellent leadership training, form an alliance, and use the media effectively. But if you don't establish group morale, all of these things we be in vain.

We can even make the case that all successful organizations have morale. And believe me; you will know morale when you see it. Organizations with high morale have well-attended meetings and events. Members of such organizations proudly identify with the group, are aware of its general activities and issues, and will readily identify the organization verbally and via editorials in the newspaper. Members in high-morale organizations will wear hats, t-shirts and buttons identifying their affiliation with the group and willingly participate in organizational functions, rallies and demonstrations.

As you can see, morale plays a vital role in an organization. Fortunately for us, morale is not a mystical or magical phenomenon. Nor is it innate to an organization.

In fact, morale is something that the leadership/Executive Board of a Black Student Union can *strategically cultivate* within their membership. Generally, an organization cultivates internal enthusiasm, loyalty and respect among members in a variety of ways, by providing for example: 1. excellent programming 2. Inspiring, informative and engaging meetings 3. A clearly conveyed organizational purpose/mission 4. Consistent displays of respect and integrity from the leadership. We've already addressed points 1-3 at length. Point 4 deserves more elaboration.

We tend to respect and appreciate people that listen to us, ask us for our input, tell us the truth, assist us, and treat us with respect. The same holds true for how we relate to organizations or businesses.

Imagine that you visit a clothing store and have difficulty finding an outfit that fits well, looks nice and fits your budget. A store clerk notifies you of a tremendous sale and takes you to another section of the store where you find clothing you like. You are impressed when a clerk in a department store provides you with good service, going out of his/her way to assist you. When this is coupled with excellent products and affordable prices, you will most likely do repeat business with that store and encourage your friends to do so.

Now let's change the scenario. You visit a store and have to wait a long time before being served. A security clerk trails behind you closely observing your actions everywhere you go (a situation many Black shoppers can relate to). Your sales clerk never looks you in the eye, acts like they're doing YOU a favor, and speaks to you rudely. You will NOT do business again in that store, and will probably spread that message to your friends.

If you understand this, you will also understand the role that a BSUs interaction with members plays in building (or destroying) morale. Therefore, we conclude this chapter with the following guidelines for BSU leadership (in addition to excellent programming, engaging meetings, and articulating a clear BSU mission):

- All officers should treat members with respect and a degree of professionalism

- BSU members deserve to be listened to whether we agree or not

- Arguing or fighting with members is strictly prohibited

- The campus BSU is there to serve and advance Black students. When a member enters the BSU office, they should not find you in there playing spades, telling inappropriate or distasteful jokes, or trying to sexually proposition them. Members should feel safe and comfortable in the BSU office, in BSU meetings, and at BSU events

- The BSU should openly solicit and encourage input from its membership; BSU should not be an elitist or top-down organization

- BSU leaders should distinguish themselves by being truthful and courteous when dealing with the membership

- BSU leaders CANNOT use the organization as their personal dating station. The personal integrity/reputation of BSU leaders can make or break the organization

- The BSU should in general, make Black students proud and should improve the campus in ways that benefit them. Every excellent event, speaker, article and successful campus campaign launched by the BSU contributes exponentially to the morale of membership.

10

BSU Elections

All universities establish criteria that determine students' eligibility to run for office in student organizations. These typically include having a minimum established grade point average, being a full-time student, getting a certain number of signatures from other students on a petition supporting your candidacy, etc.

Next, candidates participate in electoral debates. These events provide general members an opportunity to question candidates for each office. Candidates use this time to establish their qualifications and experience for the position they seek and describe his/her platform and vision for the organization.

BSU leaders absolutely must take the election process seriously. Elections are not just a formality we participate in because the university says we must. Elections usher in a new wave of leadership for the BSU. With this in mind, here are some things BSU leaders should strongly consider regarding their electoral process:

- Election and debate procedures should be written and included in the BSU Constitution or By Laws to avoid any confusion. If you're Constitution does not include such procedures, amend it immediately to make sure it does.

- The actual procedure for voting must have integrity. Take *all reasonable precautions* to make sure your elections leave no room for corruption or sabotage. For example, voting should be secretive, and properly secured to make sure no one tampers with votes or attempts to vote multiple times. To prevent any perception (or practice) of favoritism or unfair influence, no BSU official should even be in the room with the ballot box. Trusted and active BSU members can handle and count votes. BSU officials also should be prohibited from speaking about candidates anywhere near the voting site. The BSU advisor is a good person to

Monitor/supervise elections and assist in tabulating votes.

- BSU elections must be advertised widely using the BSU newspaper, campus newspaper, BSU social media, campus-wide fliers, etc. No one should be able to say that the BSU leadership purposely kept elections secretive to manipulate who wins. Similarly, debates should be widely advertised.

- BSU debates should occur on at least three different dates to allow most members to attend, ask questions, and observe the candidates.

- As I suggested in the chapter on leadership training, anyone interested in running for office should be required to complete BSU leadership prior to running. This insures that every candidate is properly prepared to assume leadership. Again, this training might take place online, to accommodate student's schedules. Upon completing the training, each student would need to print out a certificate of confirmation

- Once votes are tabulated for each candidate, the voting volunteers should create a simple table that shows how many votes each candidate received, and this information should be confidential until it's posted in the BSU newspaper or official social media site

Again, BSU leaders must take their elections *seriously* and conduct them with the highest level of integrity. What is at stake, you may ask? Response: The effectiveness of your leadership transition and the consistency and legacy of your organization. Years of effective activism and organizational growth can literally be erased or discontinued due to a poorly run election.

Making Decisions

Every individual and organization is in a sense, a culmination of their decisions. We increase our effectiveness and power every time we make good decisions that are beneficial to ourselves and our group. Therefore, one of the most important tasks of leadership is getting into the habit of making consistently good choices in terms of policy, events, and how we respond to situations.

Given the gravity of this task, it is ironic that so little attention is paid to the process of making good BSU decisions. If we are honest, we'll have to admit that almost no one, student, faculty member or otherwise taught us HOW to make good decisions, or the thinking involved in doing so. This chapter attempts to do precisely this. How? Through exploring a common game!

My father introduced me to the game of chess around the time I was in the fifth grade. I was completely mesmerized and fascinated by the game, especially its interesting pieces and the unique ways that they moved. At that stage of my development, that's about all my dad could teach me.

Years later, as a high school and later college student, I viewed chess as a wonderful game of sophisticated strategy, that involved positioning, traps, pins, forks, pawn structure and critical thinking. As a public schoolteacher in NYC and an activist, I realized that the same thinking used by good chess players could apply to making life and organizational decisions. Every serious chess player asks themselves a series of questions throughout the game, both from an offensive (proactive) and defensive (reactive) point of view. Computer games and highly skilled players ask and answer these questions accurately and very quickly.

But whether we aim to become chess Grandmasters, live quality lives, or be effective leaders, this strategic thinking is useful. If you apply this thinking, your decisions will tend to be sounder, and they will bring honor and success to your BSU more often than not.

I am not alone in this assessment. Based on studies that show dramatic improvement in critical thinking, problem-solving and decision-making, approximately 30 countries include chess in their elementary school curriculums!

The problem with many people is that they approach life like a game of checkers. What you will soon understand is that life works a lot more like the game of chess. To understand this, you must recognize the difference between the two games.

Checkers is a fast-paced game that is usually over in less than 15 minutes. The pieces all basically move the same, and therefore, your options are very limited. Moves are usually made very quickly and typically without much thought. Also, the objective of the game is very simple: you win by capturing all of your opponent's pieces.

Chess is completely different. In chess, there are eight distinct pieces which are assigned different relative values for the purpose of assisting players with making sacrifices and trades. (Pawns are worth 1 point, Knights and Bishops 3, Rooks 5, and the Queen is worth 9 points. Since the King cannot be captured or traded in a game its value has no standard designation).

Chess pieces are different from checkers pieces in their mobility as well. Some move vertically and horizontally, others along diagonal lines, and in the case of the Queen, a combination of all the above.

And unlike in the game of checkers, where the moves and possibilities are limited, after just 5 moves in chess, there are more than 4 million possible positions! Chess therefore, is a much more complex and nuanced game.

Chess is a game that requires you to think several moves ahead. In checkers, you usually think about your next move. In chess, the very best players think as much as 20 moves ahead. Now that's some serious thinking! Because chess is so complex, a game could last anywhere from 5 minutes to over an hour depending on the skill level of the players.

Of all the games in existence, chess is most like life because it involves having sound strategy, understanding rules, and making decisions that benefit you in the future.

So how can you think like a chess player even if you never played the game? A good chess player asks several questions during the course of the game. If you train yourself to ask similar questions before making a decision in life, your decisions are more likely to result in good results. There are some typical questions a chess player must ask herself before making a move.

A good chess player asks the right questions, comes up with the right answers, and then makes the best moves based on those answers. Everything he/she does is well planned and designed to establish a specific result.

In a typical chess game a player might ask themselves dozens or even hundreds of questions, but most are variations of the following. Below are the most common questions that good chess players ask during the course of a game. Please note that "piece" can also mean resource, advantage, or momentum when referring to real life. If you teach yourself to ask similar questions relevant to your organization and people with whom you interact, your decisions will become more sound and rewarding.

Defensive questions (in response to an opponent's moves):

- What is this person's objective or motivation?
- How does this affect me?
- Is he/she attacking any of my pieces?
- Are my pieces protected?
- If I lose a piece and respond by capturing my opponent's piece, is this an exchange that benefits me or causes me disadvantage?
- Why did he/she make that particular move? (I.e. To gain position, launch an attack, protect oneself, divert my attention from a current attack)

- Will my intended response help me gain or lose momentum?
- Is there a move I can make that will defend my pieces and attack his/her pieces simultaneously?
- What move can I make to neutralize his/her specific attack or general strategy?
- My opponent's last move allows me to capture one of his/her pieces. Was this an innocent mistake or a trap? Will capturing this piece strengthen or weaken my general position?

Offensive questions (that initiate an attack or that are proactive):

- What are my general strategy objectives?
- Will my intended move improve my position on the board, attack my opponent or force them to temporarily abandon or frustrate their strategy?
- What is my assessment of my and my opponent's situation at this point in the game? (Whose pieces are better positioned? Who has more power pieces on the board? Which pieces have already been captured? Am I are or is my opponent close to being checkmated? Do any pawns threaten to reach the other side? Are all of my pieces protected? Are any of my opponent's pieces vulnerable to attack?)

- Will my next move gain or lose time? (Will I be able to develop new pieces, or will I be forced to reposition the piece I just moved?
- Is there a better move to make?
- How can I make moves that allow me to spend less time and energy to achieve my objective?
- How will my opponent likely respond to my move? How should I respond to or neutralize his/her anticipated moves?

- Can I sacrifice a piece to gain better position or divert his/her attention from my attack?
- Can I put my opponent in check or end the game with checkmate?

Please remember that I'm using chess as an analogy here and this analogy is not a perfect fit in the real world of politics. The language I used refers to "pieces," "opponent," a "board," "position," "defense" and "attack." As a student leader, hostile organizations or unresponsive university officials might be your "opposition." Additionally, situations, people or problems to solve might be seen as opponents. Your "pieces" on campus can be your membership, resources, and alliances. Defense translates to protecting the BSU's image, resources, or political interests/actions. At this point, the questions I identified are quite abstract. Let's examine some of the questions I noted above in real time by exploring how they fit into actual scenarios you may face as a student leader. I should add that I or someone I know faced each of these scenarios during my tenure as a BSU President.

Scenario #1: A radical and controversial feminist or gay student group asks you as BSU President to speak at their rally in support of a policy they advocate. You must weigh this decision carefully.

Your presence and the things you say publically represent the BSU. Therefore, you'll want to ask yourself some "defensive" questions before accepting or rejecting this invitation. Why did they ask YOU to speak at the rally? What does YOUR participation mean to them? How does your support benefit them? Does this policy they want you to support coincide with the BSUs purpose? Is it consistent with or contradictory to your purpose? Will it depict your organization in a favorable light or a negative one? To what extent does the policy you may support positively or negatively affect your constituents? The final decision is the BSUs to make. However you should consider these things prior to making a decision

Scenario #2: Your constitution calls for you as president to have a personal assistant or secretary whom you appoint. You announce this at your last BSU general meeting. Your girlfriend or boyfriend (whom you virtually live with and who is also active in the BSU) wants you to appoint him/her to the position. This is an innocent request and an easy decision, right?

It might appear to be, but because it could possibly affect your organization you should enter decision mode and ask yourself questions like these: Does he/she actually meet the requirements for the position? Are you confident he/she would perform their tasks well? How might members of the BSU perceive you and your leadership if you appoint your boyfriend/girlfriend? (I.e. might they see this as a form of nepotism? Will they see this as a possible conflict of interests? Will they see your appointment as an unfair and biased one, and therefore perceive you as a weak and self-absorbed leader?)

Will personal issues/conflicts between you and your lover leak into and affect the organization? I will not advise you here about what to choose, but instead stress that you raise important questions to arrive at a sound leadership decision.

Scenario 3: A Black sorority sister on campus accuses a popular Black fraternity of gang raping her one evening. A very worried and upset member of this fraternity (who you are cool with) asks to meet with you and informs you of the charge, insisting that the young lady is dishonest; According to him, she not only consented to the sexual activity, but actually arranged it. In lieu of the young lady's accusation, the university prohibits fraternity members in question from being on campus unless there for school related business. He feels this is unfair and wants you as BSU president to get involved in the situation, which will hopefully clear his fraternity of the charges.

Before answering him, you should take some time to ponder the issue. Questions you might ask, include: Does this issue fall under the purpose of your organization? Does the BSU have jurisdiction or influence on a criminal charge like this? How will supporting this fraternity read to the woman that made the charge, to other Black sororities or all of your female members? Do you know or can you prove that these brothers are innocent? Is there already a university procedure in place to address this issue? How would support for the accused fraternity affect your campus and community image? What BSU resources are needed to support the fraternity? Can the organization afford to use these resources in this manner? Will your executive board and general membership likely support this move? Can the fraternity seek help from their national chapter or Pan Hellenic Council?

These scenarios are included to help you understand how to incorporate the system of questioning mentioned earlier. In a larger sense, this is one of the most important chapters of this book, because effective leadership CANNOT exist without good decision-making. I believe one's life is essentially a culmination of choices they make. Therefore, the chess player's approach to making decisions is good not only for people in leadership positions, but people in general. Thinking in this manner is the foundation of strategic vs. impulsive decisions and actions.

Maintaining Archives

Malcolm X once noted that "A person without history is like a tree without roots." The same is true for organizations. The BSUs purpose and objectives, traditions, annual events and significant triumphs and even mistakes all form part of its history.

Organizational history is important to a BSU for it provides a record of past activities. Such history becomes a powerful tool to evaluate and sharpen organizational objectives. We can review our history to evaluate and compare different BSU administrations, review and build upon past victories, and avoid past mistakes.

Yet how will current and future BSU members know and utilize their history if no one bothers to record and store it? This chapter will outline how to maintain good historical archives.

As a graduate student at Cornell University, I frequently visited the university's archives while doing research for my Master's thesis (which dealt in part, with the Black student movement to create a Black Studies Department at Cornell in 1968-69). I pored over hundreds of private letters, BSU documents, newspaper clippings, and transcribed interviews.

What most impressed me was: 1. that the university actually kept all those boxes of old information and 2. The great care utilized in keeping the material. All visitors to the archives had to place their bags in a locker before entering. We had to wear thin gloves provided by the staff to prevent leaving fingerprints or smudges on documents. The documents were often copied on special archival paper that resisted the oxidation (yellowing) often associated with age and exposure to light. Furthermore, no visitor could take original documents out of the archive, only copies.

We can't expect college Black Student Unions to live up to the same practices as an Ivy League university. Yet we can learn from their example. We too, must take special care to record and maintain the history of our organizations, and to do so in a way that makes such history useful to BSU leaders and constituents.

Any BSU member or alum should be able to visit your archive and research BSU activities, administrations and general history from various years. Too often, BSU offices have missing articles, and poorly maintained and categorized materials. Given the importance of this task, I'd like to suggest that all BSUs around the country and world create a new "archivist" or historian position. This office might be a position appointed by the president. This officer's sole task is to document, categorize and safely store all BSU material deemed relevant. This "material" includes pictures/video of events, constitutions, BSU newsletters, community and campus newspaper clippings featuring BSU leaders and activities, posters, fliers, press releases, official letters written by BSU officials, etc.

General Guidelines

- The archivist must make a special effort to maintain a hard copy file, digitized picture files, and pdf files and have these backed up on an Internet service like *Drop box*

- All print material to the degree possible should be copied onto *archival* paper

- All physical files should be categorized by content, topic, or when applicable, names of people

- Files should be backed up on a portable hard drive

- When storing backup files on the internet, the archivist must provide the BSU President with all or any passwords needed for access

- The archivist must either be present or arrange for someone to be present at all BSU events and should assemble a committee to assist with photography, videography, news clippings, etc.

- Newspaper files should be stored in chronological order by month and year

- Articles that have anything to do with the organization, including critiques of the BSU or materials demonstrating BSU errors/defeats must be chronicled as well. In other words, the history you record and store must be balanced, comprehensive and objective

- Safety is a key word here. The archivist must consider ways to protect BSU archives from age, light, humidity, temperature, desecration, and theft. At a minimum, key pictures should be scanned and saved as digital files, paper documents should be kept in archival safe acid-free plastic sleeves.

Needless to say, all archival material should be stored in a locked file cabinet.

The Anatomy of a Movement

By "movement," I'm referring to a sustained and organized struggle on behalf of a group that demands concessions from an agency/institution. This assumes an adversarial or contentious relationship between two parties like the BSU and the university for example. The BSU wants a certain thing or set of things which the university can provide but refuses to for any number of reasons. Therefore the BSU launches a movement or campaign to get the concessions it wants.

I began this book expressing disappointment with those BSUs around the country that have become social clubs rather than the agents of resistance and empowerment they were founded to be. My hope is that this book has inspired a return to that BSU spirit. This chapter will equip your organization to take its rightful place in the tradition of BSUs by acquainting you with the "anatomy" so to speak, of a movement.

We might say that a movement is composed of 8 general parts: *Irreconcilable Discontent, Research, Propaganda,* a *Call to action, Presentation of demands, Outreach & Alliance Building, Confrontation,* and *Negotiation.*

Irreconcilable Discontent: This refers to a mentality or psychological state which leads people to create a movement to confront the university or any other power structure. People may experience discontent with a situation for several years but never do anything to resolve their conflicts because they have "made peace" with it in one way or another. They might rationalize that this "is just the way things are," or that "we can't win" or refuse to seriously address the issue out of fear or personal discomfort.

But *irreconcilable* discontent takes place when an incident occurs that is so egregious, so blatantly insulting or oppressive that people overcome their fears and skepticism and feel *compelled* to respond in organized fashion. For example, Black people have resented the ominous presence and brutal activities of police in our communities for decades. We detest police harassing Black motorists, stopping and frisking our youth, and shooting us down in the streets. We know this is unjust and criminal; we know that the officers responsible go free and resume their presence on the police force. Yet despite our discontent we reconcile with such practices, telling ourselves to "let the system do its job," or that "God will punish them." As demonstrated in our response to Trayvon Martin's murder on February 26, 2012, and his murderer's subsequent exoneration, we participate in a few marches or petition drives, hold some press conferences and rallies, and eventually go back to business as usual. Irreconcilable discontent means "the straw has broken the camel's back," we come to the realization that "Enough is enough," and we are compelled to act in an assertive manner (even to the point of breaking oppressive rules/laws and refusing to cooperate with societal convention).

In Montgomery, Alabama, Black people in the 1950s were accustomed to sitting in the segregated section of the bus. We were accustomed to paying our fare, then exiting to board the bus via the back door. Often the bus drivers pulled off with us standing there. We didn't like this mistreatment. We were discontented, for sure, but we mumbled under our breath, accepting that this obvious form of injustice was "just the way things were" at that time. Of course some individuals refused to comply with the segregation laws, but Blacks did not collectively wage a movement.

But when innocent and well-respected seamstress Rosa Parks was roughly taken off the bus and arrested for not complying with the law, Blacks in Montgomery became *irreconcilably discontented*. And this sense of outrage led to a 381 day bus boycott that nearly brought the bus company to bankruptcy and led to a court decision banning bus segregation.

Successful campaigns or movements almost always begin when our people feel a sense of outrage so intense that they are ready and willing to take action. **Astute leaders recognize such moments and begin organizing this widespread anger and frustration into a sustained and organized movement for social or political change**.

Research: At some point, organizers and activists begin researching to determine who is responsible for resolving the issue, methods they can take to bring attention to the issue, and what specific demands they will make to the parties that have the power to resolve the issue.

Call to Action: Having defined the issues, and "opposition force" responsible for resolving them, the organizers and activists issue a call to action to the masses, directly calling upon them to move beyond discontent and into organized action. During this early phase of your movement, you will hold meetings with your group to effectively explain how this issue affects your members, why they should be outraged, and give them a sense of their power to resolve the issue.

Presentation of Demands: After concluding your research to clarify the issues involved and party responsible, you formally present your grievances and demands to the responsible party. You can do this in several ways, including a petition, letter, or verbally at a meeting with the person you identify as the responsible party. This is obviously the main goal of your movement, namely to get your demands satisfied. In the best case, your demands are agreed to in writing. This is not very likely to happen however, as powerful organizations tend to underestimate your seriousness or validity of your cause and do not respond well to changing their policies/practices or spending money to resolve your conflicts.

Outreach & Alliance Building: Anticipating a long struggle, your organization contacts other groups and leaders for support and resources to assist you. This lends greater numbers and therefore strength to your cause. You want to identify campus and community organizations to support you. If you've been building relations with these people in advance (as I suggested earlier) this step will prove easier and more successful.

Propaganda: In an effort to heighten and dramatize the tension surrounding the issue, organizers use propaganda. Through informational fliers, press conferences and rallies, they use colorful language and imagery to expose the contradictions involved, highlight the specific injustice(s), and call for the responsible parties to take corrective action. Your propaganda should powerfully describe and detail the injustice, identify your grievances and demands, and explain how and why your demands went unmet.

During this phase it's important that the organization identify an individual as their opposition or responsible party. A corporation, university or other institution might be responsible, but you must put a face on that institution, as people cannot effectively confront an abstract "company." Your research should have discovered one person (a CEO, university president, or elected official who is representative of the organization you're going to confront). During this phase, you'll want to write editorials in your college, organization and community newspapers and give press conferences detailing your issue. You want everyone to clearly understand what you're fighting for and how it impacts you and others.

Confrontation: In this phase of the movement or campaign the disgruntled organization directly confronts the individual (representative of the institution) believed to be responsible for creating or at least resolving the issue. Naturally, this only occurs if your grievances and demands are initially unmet. To encourage sympathy from outside observers and to develop proper momentum, you should begin with simple, less intense and more "respectable" tactics (petitions, meetings, rallies, newspaper articles) and if necessary, become increasingly more intense, dramatic and aggressive.

If the opposition doesn't respond to these tactics and you're compelled to engage in more assertive measures, other people not involved in your movement will more likely understand and support your cause as being fair and reasonable. They will also be more likely to view your opposition as being unreasonable and unfair. This perception and sympathy may come in handy later in your campaign when you need all the outside support you can get. When your tactics become more aggressive, the court of public opinion will be likely be in your favor.

Confrontations typically consist of specific tactics. These may include petitions, letter-writing campaigns, rallies, building takeovers, marches, mass phone calls of complaint/concern to the individual/institution, and demonstrations and protests.

Petitions are concise letters that clearly specify the issues involved, your grievances and demands, and the person/institution you deem responsible for addressing your issue. These letters have space at the bottom for your supporters to sign in agreement with your petition demands.

The strength of a petition lies in the number of people that sign it. It shows that your organization has a large and diverse base of support, and puts pressure on the opposition to take your matter seriously and to resolve it. Because each person that signs your petition reads it first, a petition is also an excellent way to inform the public about your organization and the issue you're fighting for. Petition drives often result in people joining or becoming supportive of your organization. A petition puts the opposition on notice that you are in disagreement with a policy, procedure or situation so that they cannot claim ignorance later. It also creates a documented record of your dispute. A well orchestrated petition drive will often lead to a meeting with the opposition and in the best case, concessions from the opposition. Online petitions which you can create for free on websites like Change.org, Petitiononline.com, or ipetitions.com are powerful petition tools, because people can "sign" them with a click of a button and you can arrange it so that every time a person signs, a copy of the petition is emailed to the establishment person you designate.

Letter-writing campaigns constitute another good tactic because they get people involved in your movement and demonstrate your wide base of support. With this tactic, you provide people with a sample of the issues, injustice involved, and your grievance/demands and allow them to craft a brief letter supporting your cause. These days, you would most likely use email to accomplish this.

Rallies are (usually) outdoor meetings held in a high-traffic area on campus or in the community. You have various leaders and activists from your group and others speak on your movement and what you're fighting for. Your primary goal is to educate the public and generate support. For added effectiveness, you can have tables at your rally site where people sign your petitions or receive more information about your organization. These types of events tend to attract media coverage which promotes your movement to people who know little or nothing about it. You'll want to invite powerful and informed speakers who are respected by the community and list their names on your fliers promoting the event. Their followers and supporters will come to hear them speak which helps you gain even more supporters. Effective rallies are informative and dynamic. The audience should be encouraged to chant (i.e. "No justice, no peace!" "A people united will never be defeated") sing protest songs hold signs and applaud loudly.

Building Takeovers are forms of protest that are very dramatic, controversial, attention-grabbing, and usually illegal. But because this involves disrupting a place of business and because it is potentially intimidating to workers in the building, this tactic is risky. It can create enemies among innocent workers who may not understand or agree with your issue, brand your organization as violent or coercive, and lead to the destruction of property or even minor injuries. Takeovers are generally banned by institutions so you face the very real likelihood of arrests. This tactic MUST be well-organized and you must clearly communicate dos and don'ts for your participants or this can backfire in very negative ways for your movement.

Marches involve a large number of people walking in unison to a designated place where an organization usually holds a rally. Marches are accompanied by colorful signs with headlines that dramatize your issue. You can organize singing and chanting as people march or do a silent march. These are excellent for generating media coverage and attracting the attention of passers-by who wonder what all the commotion is about. Because they involve large audiences, march conveners should make sure the event is well-organized. You must inform participants beforehand what route they will use, what the destination is and what the issue is. Also, you should have a spokesperson on hand to speak with reporters and answer questions.

Mass phone calls are self-explanatory. You provide hundreds of people with the work phone number of your opposition figure (calling their home or cell phone might be seen as a form of harassment) and a few basic scripts to read when the person (or their assistant) answers. Each person calls and explains his/her concern about your issue. Then they ask what this person or office plans to do about it. This is a legal and completely easy way to disrupt the individual's work day while reinforcing your issue. When done correctly, this tactic ties up your opposition's phone lines and makes it difficult for them to conduct business as usual. Even if no one answers, your callers can leave a message. This pressure tactic demonstrates your strength and wide base of support. It also subtly pressures them to resolve your issue in an effort to return to their orderly business. I like to call this tactic 'Holding the phone lines hostage."

Demonstrations represent another dramatic tactic which draw media coverage for your issue and involve great fun. You can think of a demonstration as social theater. People using this tactic dramatize the said issue in very creative and engaging ways designed to describe (in exaggerated fashion) exactly why and how the institution, policy or practice is oppressive, exploitive or simply unfair.

Students protesting a tuition hike might stage a demonstration in which a college class has a professor lecturing to only three students who happen to be wealthy and pampered. This is designed to illustrate the organization's belief that the proposed tuition increase will significantly reduce the student population and make the college affordable only to affluent students.

A BSU protesting a policy that ends affirmative action on their campus might stage a funeral scene. Pallbearers solemnly carry a casket marked "Black Students at this university." Once inside the mock funeral home, the preacher begins to deliver a moving eulogy for Black students on campus, noting that the removal of affirmative action "killed" the presence of Blacks on campus. Nearby, in a mock court scene, we see a prosecutor grilling the university president and accusing him of "murdering" affirmative action. A Black-student jury pronounces him guilty and the mock university president is led out of court in handcuffs. As you might imagine, these demonstrations dramatize the perceived injustices involved in ways that are more fun and sensational than would be the case using a rally or petition drive. They also guarantee media coverage and depict the opposition in a negative light. By definition, demonstrations involve the skillful use of propaganda.

Negotiation: Usually the last phase of a successful campaign involves a series of meetings between a BSU representative (usually the president and a Vice President) and a representative of the opposition. At this point, the institution has suffered great embarrassment in the media and tremendous pressure from the BSU and its supporters. In an effort to continue operating normally and end its public embarrassment and increasingly aggressive BSU protests and demonstrations, the opposing institution is now compelled to sit with your organization to bring the movement to an end by making concessions.

In most cases, the negotiating phase involves some degree of compromise and flexibility from the protesting organization. Sometimes budgetary considerations or other realities make some demands untenable or impractical. In these cases, the BSU will have to determine which demands are most important and non-negotiable. After these meetings, all agreements made verbally must be put in writing and signed by a person with the authority to grant the requests and the BSU official. It is important to establish reasonable dates by which these changes will be implemented or the university has wiggle room to renege on their agreements.

In conclusion, please realize that no movement or campaign unfolds in one specific manner. This anatomy of a campaign I provided cannot possibly account for or anticipate every single nuance of a struggle. It does however acquaint you with the general things you should consider and prepare for. Now that you have an abstract or theoretical understanding of launching a struggle, I will provide you with some case studies –real events- I participated in as the president of the Student African American Society at Syracuse University, 1988-90. The purpose of exploring these activities is to help you see some of the principles/actions outlined in this book being implemented.

14

Case Study#1: *"Operation Infiltration"*

In the fall of 1990, Black students at Syracuse University faced a seemingly perennial problem. White council members of the Student Government Association (SGA) once again attempted to award the Student African American Society (SAS) a budget amount of...zero dollars.

As I implied before, this was not a new tactic. Indeed, since 1986 when I entered the university, reactionary white students tried to zero SAS' budget.

Black students were by no means naïve. We understood the persistent attack on our budget as an attempt to neutralize our powerful presence and political impact on Syracuse University. Since its birth in 1967, SAS raised and challenged pivotal issues of race and politics on campus. While this activity won ardent supporters, it also earned the wrath of some white students who resented our very presence on campus let alone our audacity to stand up and speak out.

Prior to my arrival on campus, then-SAS president Charles "Chuck" Wynder wisely sought to address the budget attack problem by becoming the Student Government Treasurer to preside over budget hearings and by leading sit-ins during the Student Government Budget hearings. Prior to that, SAS typically wrote scathing articles and conducted rallies protesting what was perceived as a SGA move to attack and disarm SAS.

Years later as SAS president, I too faced the same predicament. I met with my trusty Vice President of External Affairs, Samuel Reynolds to discuss ways to confront the issue. I recently reviewed Brother Malcolm's famous speech *Message to the Grassroots* (for the millionth time), where he urged Black people to work together despite ideological differences.

This speech gave me an epiphany, which I promptly shared with my executive board: Instead of protesting SAS' budget cut proposals after the fact, we would prevent them to begin with!

The Student Government Assembly was essentially our campus version of Congress. This body conducted budget hearings, made budget recommendations, and ultimately approved every student group's budget.

I want to emphasize that our final approach to addressing this problem was *strategic and reflective*. We developed our strategy after much deliberation. We reviewed SAS' past efforts to deal with this persistent problem; We evaluated how successful and effective past strategies were; We studied the structure of the Student Government Association, particularly the budget hearing process and the role of the Student Assembly in facilitating it. Finally, we came to the conclusion that previous SAS attempts were limited in scope and effectiveness.

Contrary to how this sounds, this was not in any way disrespectful or dismissive to previous SAS administrations. Improving on past efforts is what organizations are *supposed* to do: In the world of organizing, if you do the same thing your predecessors did, and get the same unsatisfying results, you have failed your constituents and your mandate to lead effectively!

We concluded that past approaches put us in a defensive and reactive position, and generally only succeeded in preventing our budget from being eliminated. But we were still at the mercy of the Student Government Assembly. We sought a strategy that would protect our budget, increase it, and empower us to help other Black organizations on campus do the same! Our days of protesting and sitting in were over. "Let white student groups be upset and on the defensive for a change," we thought.

Our plan was to simply fill the student assembly with a majority of Black representatives and therefore control the entire budget allocation process. This ambitious plan we believed, was a *proactive* approach in which we would utilize the very system attempting to sabotage us for our own empowerment!

After discussing this among our executive board, we called a special general SAS meeting and shared our findings with general members. We educated our general body on how SAS handled this issue in the past. Next we educated our members on how budget hearings worked and on who held the power to approve or reject budgetary requests from student organizations. Finally we put the strategy to a vote, and our constituents backed our plan unanimously! And thus our strategy – which I nicknamed "Operation Infiltration" – was born.

This is when the real work and organizing effort began. Anticipating that our constituents would approve the idea, we brought copies of a chart which showed each campus dormitory along with the number of student assembly seats designated to each dorm. This system was designed to ensure that the student assembly was representative of all students on campus. After explaining this, we suggested that our goal was to flood the student assembly with Black representatives (more specifically, those loyal to or supportive of SAS).

We therefore encouraged people present to consider running for the assembly. Next, we solicited one person per dormitory to be responsible for informing Black students in their dorm about our plan and recruiting them to participate. Everyone was asked to keep this plan confidential for obvious reasons. If whites didn't know about our plan, they couldn't sabotage it!

These point people would hold small meetings with interested Black students in their assigned dormitory, and explain the budget hearing process, the duties and powers of assembly members, the number of assembly seats available from their particular dormitory, and most importantly, SAS' objective for doing this in the first place. When possible, we had current Black assembly members come to these meetings to address these points as well from a position of experience. We even had the SGA Treasurer and SGA President (both Black men we established good relationships with) advise us on how to craft our budget and prepare for complicated questioning.

Two months later, we successfully infiltrated the SGA assembly and in fact held the majority of seats! Some whites became bitter and suspicious about this new development, and wrote scathing articles in the campus newspaper concerning SAS' "illegal and unethical" domination of the assembly elections process. But their protests were in vain; SAS committed no violation of SGA rules or regulations. Simply put, we beat them at their own game, and it was deeply satisfying to see white students protesting and upset for once!

As this process began to unfold, I held private meetings with other Black organizations on campus to advise them of our plans and to determine their budgetary requests. We asked each participating organization to provide a minimum, barebones budget in addition to a more extravagant budget. Then, we forwarded the proposed budgets for approximately 5-7 Black organizations to our newly-elected Black assembly members to make sure they had to time review them and prepare arguments to defend and approve them. Since the Black fraternity Omega Psi Phi ("Q-Dogs") owned a house on campus, we arranged to use it for holding our meetings with Black student leaders on campus.

When the much-anticipated budget hearings arrived, SAS and the other Black groups in our alliance were cool, calm and confident. In an unprecedented move, SAS and our partners received every dime we asked for, in many cases amounting to larger budget allocations than we received in previous years! "Operation Infiltration" was a complete success, and we pulled it off without one march, protest or sit-in. Rival white organizations and student leaders were dumbfounded. They could not understand how Black students out-strategized them.

I describe this campaign because it involves many of the concepts and actions I outline in this book. I'd like to highlight the more important points here to underscore the lessons I hope you gain from this and to illustrate how the points I addressed throughout this handbook come together:

✓ Realizing the importance of having enough money for programming and organizational operations, we took a *proactive* position. Namely, we refused to be in a situation where we had to protest in response to other people's actions.

✓ We *conducted research* to learn how the SGA was organized, and who held the power to approve budgets. Once we learned that assembly members held this power, we familiarized ourselves with the duties of assembly members and how they were elected.

✓ We called a general meeting to *share this information* with our constituents and to get their input on the proposed strategy. Therefore we used an inclusive rather than top-down approach and did not make any decision without their approval.

✓ Rather than trying to do everything ourselves, the SAS executive board increased the circle of leadership and shared responsibility by having individuals take the lead for recruiting Black assembly members in their respective dormitories

✓ We were able to include the SGA president and treasurer in our planning because we formed working relationships with them prior to the time that we needed their help. Their advice and assistance proved invaluable. This highlights the importance of building relationships with people and organizations on campus.

✓ By including other Black organizations in our plan, we practiced a much-discussed concept called *"Black solidarity."* We basically worked with other Black leaders and organizations around a common interest (maintaining and increasing our budgets). This unselfish move earned SAS great respect and future support from the other groups that benefitted from Operation Infiltration, and demonstrated to ourselves and others the power we had when we are organized, proactive, and strategic.

✓ By acting in a proactive manner, rather than being reactive, by helping to unify several Black organizations, by improving upon past efforts to solve a problem, and by winning our campaign and increasing the financial capacities of Black groups, we achieved and demonstrated a key goal of any BSU; To empower Black students!

Case Study #2: The Book Incident

One day during midterm examinations, two Black sorority sisters who were also active SAS constituents came into the SAS office and told me that a white male student, upset by their whispering, threw a huge history book at them and yelled, "Shut the fuck up, niggers!" While the book did not hit either of them, they were incensed by his assault and offensive language.

I shared their righteous indignation. Black students had a right to safety on campus, and SAS would make an example of this student to let it be known that we would not tolerate anyone harassing or intimidating Black students. I also believed that SAS needed to make a strong statement to our own members that we would fight for them and defend our collective interests. With these issues in mind, I made an admittedly unilateral decision to advocate for them and hold their assailant accountable for his actions. As his action clearly violated Syracuse University's honor code, I encouraged them to file a complaint with the university, but first we had to identify this student.

Fortunately the young man wore a white fraternity sweatshirt. The SAS constituents, who were members of Delta Sigma Theta sorority, recognized the Greek letters on his shirt and identified his fraternity. It so happened that this particular fraternity owned a house on Fraternity/Sorority Row, a long block of opulent white fraternity and sorority homes adjacent to campus.

The next day, the three of us went to this particular fraternity house, explained the incident and demanded to speak with the fraternity brother responsible for the assault and racial epithet. Visibly nervous, the young man that answered the door stuttered that he had no idea which of his brothers was responsible. The sisters for whom I was advocating suggested he produce a yearbook (which contained a photograph of each fraternity brother) and he complied. After visually scanning several pages, they identified the guy. We demanded that he come to the door, but were told he wasn't home. However, we got the main information we wanted – his full name.

Armed with this information, the two sorority sisters filed a complaint with the university and a hearing was set. SAS decided to do a demonstration designed to make this guy feel intimidated like he made our constituents feel when he threw the book at them. We knew the date, time and location of the hearing and planned to be there when he arrived. So I asked all SAS constituents to be at that location wearing all-black and bring the biggest textbook they could find.

On the day of the hearing, over 300 SAS members dressed in all-black, assembled shoulder-to shoulder on both sides of the long, winding walkway to the hearing building. As he approached, and on my cue, all of us held up a book, positioned as if we were going to throw it at him. We cautioned our members not to throw their books, but to stand there with their books cocked back and with serious facial expressions. I distinctly remember him turning red in embarrassment and shaking in fear as he awkwardly made his way to the hearing.

The demonstration lasted all of 2 or 3 minutes, but sent a strong message to all onlookers that SAS members would stand up for ourselves and not tolerate harassment of any kind from ANYONE. If I recall correctly, the fraternity guy was suspended from school, forced to write a public apology to our sisters in the campus newspaper, and had to write a research paper on the negative history of the N-word. Those assaulted sisters felt defended by their organization, and Black students on campus experienced a surge of morale and pride for the stand SAS took.

This might seem coercive or intimidating to those of you reading this book. Perhaps it was to some extent. But our decisive leadership, supported by powerful collective action helped Black students walk tall, defend their fellow members and feel they were part of an organization that got things done.

16

Case Study#3: The Fight for Black Studies

Of all my experiences as a BSU leader, none was more defining, educational, controversial or inspiring as SAS' campaign to strengthen and redevelop our African American Studies Department during 1988-1989. It was during this struggle that SAS distinguished itself as the most dynamic, outspoken and effective student organization at Syracuse University at the time and probably for some time to come.

In Chapter 13, we described the anatomy of a movement as including discontent, research, a call to action, outreach & alliance-building, propaganda, presentation of demands, confrontation, and negotiation. As you will see, the SAS struggle to support our AAS Department incorporates each of these components and then some.

Prior to the start of fall semester 1988, I met with the SAS Executive Board to determine what major issues we would address or concern ourselves with for the year. We wanted to decide the issues rather than have them decided for us. We decided to create a survey for our general body and to disseminate that survey at our first general meeting.

Essentially, the survey sought to determine what singular issue our members most wanted to address. The questions were:

- What issue would you most support?
- What issue most affects you?
- What issue are you most willing to sacrifice for?
- What issue do you believe will most affect future students?

After collecting and tabulating these surveys, we concluded that the number one issue our people wanted to address was the AAS Department. It made complete sense, given the condition of the Department. The Department had an interim Chairperson but no regular-appointed Chairperson for more than 2 years; The Martin Luther King Jr. Library was dilapidated. It had no librarian, was not connected to the larger university library system, was shamefully under-resourced, and   suffering great structural and archival damage when the roof caved in, consequently destroying books and artwork. In addition to these issues, the Department suffered from a serious lack of faculty and graduate teaching assistants. Its Community Folk Art Gallery was seriously under resourced, and the building provided little access for disabled students or faculty.

Research Phase

In order to mount an effective campaign against the powerful Syracuse University, we had to be informed. This meant we had to conduct targeted research. Among other things, we set out to determine:

1. Which department or individual was responsible for or had the authority to address our issue

2. What exactly were all of the problems and deficiencies with the AAS Department? Which of those problems were structural (i.e. caused by outside forces or lack of support) suffered and how did these deficiencies affect its performance and service to the campus

3. What the university's role was in terms of funding or otherwise developing the AAS Department

4. What financial, faculty and structural support the AAS Department needed as a prerequisite to fulfilling its academic and community objectives

5. What previous agreements if any, were made between the university and the AAS Department in matters concerning the Department's development, and was the university negligent in its duty regarding the AAS Department?

In addition, I continued my own personal research in leadership and organizing. I can't sufficiently express how invaluable these resources were to my development as a leader and human being. I studied Marcus Garvey from whom I learned how to think BIG and inspire people; I studied Martin Luther King from whom I learned fearlessness, strategic thinking, and moral conviction; I studied Malcolm X from whom I learned the power of historical analysis, independent thinking, and language. I also read and attempted to apply lessons from some good books on leadership including: *Rules for Radicals* by Saul Olinsky, *Organizing: a Guide for Grassroots Leaders* by Si Kahn, *Leadership Secrets of Attila the Hun* by Wess Roberts, and *Roots to Power*: A Manual for Grassroots Organizing by Lee Staples among others.

During this phase of the movement we reviewed old *Daily Orange* Issues (the official student-run newspaper of Syracuse University), interviewed

AAS faculty and former SAS leaders, and reviewed Syracuse University's Organization Chart, to determine its hierarchy of leadership. It's important to acknowledge that both the SAS executive board and general membership participated in the research phase which also involved sharing the information we obtained at SAS general meetings. It was important to make sure our general body was fully and accurately informed before continuing to the next phase

Call to Action

Next, the SAS executive board issued a call to action to our constituents and the campus-at-large in the form of an editorial article I wrote:

"The African American Studies Department – which SAS fought for in the late 60s – finds itself unable to perform its academic duties because the University has failed to provide it with the support it needs. We pay tuition and white students pay tuition. But white students have a full academic menu to choose from; they can learn about Europe and their ancestors' experiences and achievements, while we Black students are forced to eat from the garbage can of academia. Until the university remedies this discrepancy, and provides our AAS Department with the support and resources it needs to function at a high level, the Student African American Society calls upon students and faculty members to join us in pressuring the university to bring the AAS Department here to speed with its excellent peers on other campuses."

Outreach & Alliance-Building

Concurrent with this call-to-action, SAS began a campaign of outreach and alliance-building. We basically contacted and met with various sympathetic campus and community leaders to explain our issue, outline our position on the issue, and our list of demands. An important part of this process involved us specifically identifying the problems facing the AAS Department, so that these leaders would thoroughly understand and support our position. This phase of the struggle was important because it helped us develop a strong and broad-based alliance of organizations backing our cause. Within two weeks or so, we had Black ministers in Syracuse, a pacifist organization in Syracuse, a progressive Jewish organization in Syracuse, the local NAACP and Urban League, along with various campus organizations and faculty members solidly backing our cause.

In months to come members of this alliance wrote letters and made calls to university officials demanding that they concede our demands, and some spoke in support of SAS at several press conferences. Later this alliance played a pivotal role in helping us win our campaign and in protecting me from expulsion as a result of my protest activities.

Presentation of Demands

After consulting with AAS faculty members, we created a 13-point list of demands reflecting concerns of both the faculty and SAS. Some of the most important demands included more money to hire full-time Black faculty, the relocation of the MLK library, hiring of a professional librarian, handicapped accessibility to the Department, increased funds to purchase more art for the Community Folk Art Gallery and begin its rennovation, hiring a full-time Chairperson for the Department and graduate teaching assistants, creating a Master's Degree within the Department, and a study abroad program allowing students to spend a semester studying in African nations.

We presented these demands to Syracuse University Chancellor Melvin Eggers, and he suggested that neither he nor the university could address the issues anytime in the near future. We knew he would not agree to any of our demands initially. But his rejection of our demands set up the propaganda and confrontation phases of our movement. We (thinking like chess players) anticipated how the university would respond and were prepared to make our next moves.

Propaganda

After securing the base of our support from the campus and larger community, and receiving a rejection of our demands, SAS began the process of constructing and disseminating propaganda. The goal of course was to frame the issue in terms that would gain support for our cause. We wanted to depict the Chancellor and university as being selfish, unresponsive to Black students, and negligent to the AAS department. Our propaganda campaign was extensive and lasted from the beginning to the conclusion of our movement. This included:

- Posters all over campus specifying the problems concerning the AAS Dept.
- Articles in University, SAS and local community newspapers
- Political Cartoons
- Radio and Television interviews
- Meetings with Administration
- Guest Speakers
- Regular campus rallies
- Presentation of Letters of support and solidarity from community/campus organizations

We now had significant campus and community support, media coverage, and had put the university on notice regarding our demands (which they summarily rejected). We'd also done a good job of portraying the university as tyrannical administrators who did not value Black people or our history and department on campus. But university officials had not agreed to our demands. It was now time to transition to the confrontation phase.

Confrontation

As I explained in chapter 13, the confrontation phase of a movement involves a series of tactics designed to disrupt the normal operating procedures of the opposition, discredit it or impair

 its image, and generally pressure the opposition into a negotiation phase where they are willing to meet your demands. As a general rule, tactics should also be actions that participants enjoy. Our confrontation phase disrupted, discredited, and pressured the university to resolve our grievances.

Me (left) on the cover of the S.U. Alumni magazine focusing on Black student issues and activism.

We held press conferences every two weeks to discredit the university, garner support from the local community, and keep people informed on the progress of our struggle to rebuild our AAS Department. This forced the university to respond to our information and attempt to discredit it. I personally appeared on dozens of local television and radio programs to keep our issues alive in the public mind. The result of this is that the university, not we were constantly responding and reacting, which challenged their ability to plan long-term and be proactive. We had thousands of students, community members and parents call the Chancellor's Vice Chancellor's and Dean of Arts & Sciences office phones for two weeks. This tactic disrupted their ability to do business as usual, and demonstrated the widespread support SAS had for our movement. I imagine that this tactic also had an intimidation factor as well.

We held rallies weekly and sometimes on the spur-of-the-moment to embarrass, discredit and expose the university while reinforcing our position on the issue, developing campus support for our movement, and keeping the pressure on. These rallies demonstrated our solidarity and power as a student organization and – along with our propaganda campaign – put the "court of public opinion" in our favor.

Our programming played an important psychological role in the movement to rebuild the AAS Department as well. We recognized that we needed to energize our constituents and prepare them to do battle with the university. So we contacted legendary former SAS president Chuck Wynder (who by this time had graduated and was in law school) and brought him back to Syracuse to speak specifically about the AAS issue and our need to organize and protest. In fact, we made sure that *every* speaker we brought to campus during that time had an activist background and/or supported Black resistance. The money we spent on their honorariums was therefore an investment in our political movement. By the time Kwame Ture, MLK III, Khallid Muhammad, Nikki Giovanni and Chuck were done, our already amped up general members raised their energy and commitment to even higher levels.

The time eventually came when we had to take inventory of our struggle, what we had done and what was still left to do. We began this movement in September of 1989, and while we made steady progress and were gaining momentum, the university still had not agreed to our demands. It was now February of 1989. SAS participated in 5 solid months of active struggle against Syracuse University.

But now we faced a dilemma. We planned to enter the negotiation phase of our movement by April, so that we'd have two months to win our struggle prior to summer break. We understood that time was on the side of the administration, as they were long-term employees while we were students who would eventually graduate and move on. The administration understood this as well; they wanted to stall in order to allow our momentum to die over the summer.

Again thinking like chess players, we made the decision to intensify our confrontation tactics in hopes of bringing the struggle to a successful end as quickly as possible. We planned to initiate our boldest and most confrontational tactics in February and March.

Our strategy was to *force* Melvin Eggers to the negotiation table by creating tremendous pressure and increasingly bad media for the university. All institutions are vulnerable in this area, as they depend on a wholesome image to make money and conduct business. The research we conducted almost half a year earlier, told us that the Chancellor was the person to identify as the face of our opposition. He was the person charged with leading the university and its public face of leadership.

Behind the scenes however, the Syracuse University Board of Trustees held the power. It was this body of wealthy businesspeople, scholars, and members of the clergy that raised and donated funds to the university determined university rules and regulations, and *hired and fired the university chancellor.* We knew that increased protests would cause the Trustees to put pressure on the chancellor to control the situation and protect the university's image or risk getting fired.

We decided that we must escalate our protests *immediately* and turn up the pressure on Chancellor Melvin Eggers. Incidentally, our mission received serious help from a Black administrator I will not name. This high-ranking administrator was privy to university meetings, conversations and strategy. While he performed his job with excellence, he also was sympathetic to our struggle to defend the AAS Department which included faculty he respected and with whom he was friends. He and I were in constant communication. I shared our demands and issues with him to forward to the administration, and he provided us with insight into his peers' insights and plans. His intellect, wisdom and strategic mind were impeccable, and our movement would not have been as successful without his assistance. This reinforces my earlier point about developing relationships with all types of people and groups who can help you down the line.

In February of 1989, over 200 SAS constituents occupied the chancellor's student leader roundtable meeting. This was a new series of meetings that the Chancellor (Melvin Eggers) created to give the appearance that he was sensitive and responsive to students' concerns.

Our plan was for me (as an invited student leader) to attend the meeting and for SAS constituents to storm the meeting approximately 20 minutes after it began. Everything went according to plan, and we took the meeting over, boldly welcoming everyone present to "A general meeting of the Student African American Society." Totally surprised and intimidated, the Chancellor turned red, and stuttered as he collected and looked over the petitions we delivered to him demanding that the university improve our AAS Department. In an effort to reduce our constituent's possible fear or

SAS members confront Eggers
Protestors disrupt Chancellor's Round Table

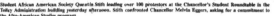

Student African American Society Quentin Stith leading over 100 protestors at the Chancellor's Student Roundtable in the Tolley Administration building yesterday afternoon. Stith confronted Chancellor Melvin Eggers, asking for a commitment to the Afro-American Studies program.

Chancellor Melvin Eggers looking at more than 100 petitions handed to him by SAS protestors.

respect of his authority, I addressed him by his first

name and then casually as "Mellie Mel." We demanded that he address the AAS issue and agree to our demands. He expressed concern for the AAS Department but mentioned that he was currently unable to respond to our demands (as we anticipated he would). We gave our constituents about 30 minutes to question Melvin Eggers about the status of the African American Studies Department, and then we promptly left.

Naturally, we contacted the campus press prior to the takeover, to insure media coverage. It tickled me to see them push their way past the Chancellor's secretary, along with us, in order to cover the takeover.

The meeting takeover was a great success. We confronted the chancellor in dramatic fashion, depicted him as a weak and indecisive leader and used the opportunity to highlight our demands while disrupting university operations and bringing bad press to the university.

However, the Chancellor still refused to agree to our demands or even hold a meeting to discuss them. Our Executive Board held several meetings to discuss how to proceed. We scheduled more rounds of rallies and press conferences to come, but knew we needed a major knockout punch, or action that would bring our struggle to an end. I and my board members entertained several ideas including a gigantic disruption of the upcoming university commencement ceremony. Our concern with this idea however, was that graduates' parents would deeply resent this action and that it would stimulate negative publicity depicting SAS as selfish, and inconsiderate of graduates and their families (some of whom were Black). Also, graduation wasn't until June, and we couldn't wait that long.

The university of course had tricks up their sleeve as well. They moved behind the scenes. My father called to tell me that the university spokesperson had called him and my mom back home in Harlem, saying that I was leading a series of protests that were embarrassing and disruptive to the university and that could result in student injuries and arrests. "I know you want your son to graduate and get his degree, but if he doesn't end his activities immediately, he might get arrested and will DEFINITELY get kicked out of school. And the university will make it difficult for him to continue his studies at any other college. So we'd like you to speak with your son and convince him to end the protests at once." My dad told me that both he and my mother told the university spokesman that they would do no such thing as they supported both SAS' cause and my activism.

Sometime in late February 1989, SAS treasurer Dina Abrams came to our E-Board meeting showing us a copy of the *Syracuse Record*. The *Record* is Syracuse University's administrative newspaper. It typically features stories about upcoming events, university business, faculty achievements, financial expenditures, and new construction activities on campus. While reading the paper, Dina noticed an article discussing an upcoming ribbon-cutting ceremony for the new Science & Technology building. The media, elected officials and business leaders were scheduled to attend. She proposed that our disruption of that event might be the knockout punch we needed.

We enthusiastically tossed the idea around, probing for its pros and cons. The major con was that it could result in student arrests or expulsions. The pros however were abundant:

- Non math, science or engineering students on campus generally resented the new building, deeming it a colossal waste of money and administrative priority. It they didn't support our protest, we believed they would at least not strongly oppose it.

- This tactic would allow us to dramatize and highlight the hypocrisy of the university who cried broke concerning the AAS Department while building a $59 million Science & Technology Center.

Dina came up with the "knockout punch" of our movement! Our constituents, who were already primed for action, loved the idea. We called a few emergency meetings in our student center, where our general body members secretly worked with us to make catchy signs with bold statements. We hid these signs in our office and instructed our members to wear all-black clothing and assemble at the student center during the late morning of March 2, 1989.

The next day approximately 500 Black students marched from the Schine student center to the ribbon-cutting ceremony where we disrupted the festivities, chastised the Chancellor for making the AAS Department such a low priority, and reiterated our demands. Predictably, the guests and the

Chancellor rushed through the ceremony once they saw us coming. Afterwards they scurried off to the luncheon. A small contingent of students stayed with me and the remainder went to the Goldstein auditorium. They'd heard invited guests talking about "going to the luncheon." This was news to us, so I asked our members to make their way to the luncheon as well.

After rallying and speaking with the media for about 5 minutes, we went to join the rest of our organization members at the luncheon, and found members of the Syracuse University Campus Security blocking our way into the auditorium. We broke up into smaller groups to attempt entry at other doors and eventually stormed into the auditorium where our other constituents awaited us.

I walked past all of the dignitaries eating, drinking, and chatting, on my way to the stage. Chancellor Melvin Eggers was seated at a table on the stage. I forcefully snatched the microphone out of his hand and said to everyone in the auditorium, "Welcome business leaders, elected officials, professors and Chancellor Melvin Eggers, to the general meeting of the Student African American Society!"

At this point, I reiterated the university's shamefully negligent position towards the AAS Department, enumerated the problems with the Department, outlined all SAS had done to move the university to address these problems, and asked the Chancellor what he would do about it. His spirit was clearly broken. He'd been personally humiliated in a most public manner in front of distinguished guests (and according to our insider, continued to face scrutiny from his Board of Trustees).

We encouraged our graduating seniors to come up to the microphone and share their feelings about the AAS Department and their experiences as Black students at Syracuse University to all present.

About 35 minutes later, after consulting with the Black administrator who sympathized with SAS, we arranged a meeting with Chancellor Eggers, which

Me (with microphone) confronting Syracuse University Chancellor (lower left), after disrupting luncheon in Goldstein Auditorium, March 2, 1989.

moved us finally into the last phase of the movement: negotiation. This was clearly a minor victory as it appeared that our last tactic achieved the negotiating meeting we wanted, earlier than the time we hoped for.

Negotiation

The university's negotiating team consisted of Chancellor Eggers, Vice Chancellor of Academic Affairs Gershon Vincow, and Dean of Arts & Sciences, Samuel Gorovitz. SAS' team was comprised of Vice President of External Affairs Samuel Reynolds, and me.

To ensure that we had the upper-hand over the university administrators, we refused to hold these meetings on territory where they felt empowered and comfortable. We instead held negotiation meetings in the Omega Psi Phi ("Q-Dogs") house on campus. We also had a larger strategy going into these meetings. We knew that the Trustees were pressuring the Chancellor to end our embarrassing and disruptive protests. They feared the continuing damage to their image. Therefore they had every incentive to resolve the situation quickly now that we delivered our knockout punch. We wanted them to agree to all of our demands without exception. Therefore, Sam would play good cop and me, bad cop. Any time the Chancellor refused even one of our demands, I would end the meeting and ask them to leave. Our first two meetings lasted a total of 10 minutes each. Imagine what went through their minds. "This will never end!"

This tactic was risky, but it put maximum pressure on the Chancellor, who had to then meet with the Board of Trustees with no progress to report. It also put pressure on the Trustees to give the Chancellor authority to concede to all our demands. Every time they asked him why he couldn't bring closure to the issue, he had to tell them that SAS wouldn't stop protesting until all of their demands were met.

By the fourth meeting of the second week after the luncheon takeover, they finally caved in and agreed to all 13 demands. We had the Chancellor initial each demand and sign his name (with a pen we provided) after the 13th point. SAS won! After a 7-month struggle, we finally got the university to commit to our AAS Department! But the struggle was still not over.

Activists must always realize that when we defeat a powerful opposition force, the opposition is often angry, resentful and embarrassed. Even when we execute a successful movement, the opposition will seek revenge and retribution. In our case, the opposition was all white middle-aged men and experienced university administrators who were out-strategized by young, Black undergraduates. Our actions put their prestige and even their reputations and jobs on the line.

Therefore SAS was not surprised when I, Samuel, and former SAS president who assisted in our movement, Ayesha Wilson, received letters from the university charging us with various violations about a week after we negotiated our demands! Naturally, the university leveled the most severe charges at me, as I was the spokesperson of SAS and the most visible and outspoken representative at rallies, protests and in interviews. If I recall correctly, they charged me with destroying university property, inciting students to riot, and injuring university staff (school safety officers). Every one of those charges was false. Nevertheless, I had to answer to them at a university hearing, and if found guilty, I would be expelled from school.

SAS immediately held a press conference informing the public of these charges. We had members of our alliance – professors and community leaders there to show their support for us. The university, though the mouth of its spokesperson, promptly held their own press conference and suggested that we were lying. According to the university, they did not file charges against us. This was easy to disprove because we had letters written on university letterhead enumerating the charges. So even though we defeated our opposition, we now had to continue holding rallies and press conferences to defend SAS leaders.

The hearing was scheduled about a week before my birthday in April. As the date approached, I grew anxious. I in no way regretted my leadership and involvement in our movement, but I'd be lying if I said I wasn't worried about being kicked out of school. Then on the day of the hearing, the Dean of Student Affairs found me in the SAS office and handed me an envelope. I was waiting for the time to go to the hearing. He told me that all charges against me, Samuel and Ayesha were dropped! When I asked why, he said- as if disappointed - that not one faculty, student or community member of the university's hearing board showed up for the hearing. In other words, all the work SAS had done months before in establishing relationships, community outreach and explaining our cause paid off. By not attending that hearing, all of these people made a powerful statement that they supported our cause! So in addition to mounting a successful campus movement and getting all of our demands met, we also avoided punishment and persecution!

I became a famous (or infamous) campus leader and local legend of sorts, and SAS gained a reputation for being a powerful and effective organization to reckon with on campus. And all of this occurred because we were strategic, proactive and followed much of the advice I've provided in this handbook.

16

Evaluating Your Leadership

Creating or joining a Black organization is one thing. Leading one is another; Leading one effectively is another matter altogether. An important part of the process involves *evaluation*. By this I refer to an accurate way of determining if we are leading effectively. Without a reliable evaluation method, we have no way of determining where our organizations stand or if they are successful.

This chapter will attempt to create a very basic form of leadership evaluation using questions in various themes. A more thorough method would involve scoring each section and would establish a range of scores representing poor, average, good and exceptional designations (this method is, as I explained, *basic and leaves room for elaboration and expansion*). However I do believe this battery of questions can help us to drastically evaluate and improve our organizations.

VISION/MISSION: A measurement of how successful we are in communicating our organization purpose and objectives

1. Do we have a clear vision of our purpose and the people we serve?

2. Do we have a clear sense of how we fulfill our purpose?

3. Are both of these clearly worded, written and distributed/taught to our members?

4. Do our members demonstrate an accurate knowledge of the vision and mission?

INTEGRITY: A measurement of the extent to which what our organization does aligns with its stated objectives/values.

1. Do our group meetings, programs/events, decisions, expenditures, and issues we raise/address coincide with, reinforce and advocate our stated vision purpose, and the people we serve?

2. What is our membership's opinion on the previous question?

3. Are leaders taught to make organizational decisions based on the organization's vision and mission?

TRAINING: A measurement of how successful we are in building leadership capacity within our organization.

1. Does our group have a formal process for identifying and grooming/mentoring new leadership and building leadership capacity?

2. Does this process work? Do the people we train demonstrate they have the skills, habits and knowledge needed to effectively lead the group?

3. Do we provide hands-on opportunities for such people to grow into effective leaders?

4. Is our training both theoretical and practical?

5. Do we delegate responsibility in ways that develop important leadership skills and experience?

ARCHIVES: Measuring how effective we are in recording, storing, and using our organization's history.

1. Does our organization have a historian or archivist responsible for recording and storing events and documents?

2. Do we have a way of determining what material is relevant to record and keep?

3. Do we make audiovisual recordings of our programs, speakers and events?

4. Do we use various means of storing important recordings, documents, and photographs (physical file cabinets, online storage)?

5. Does our membership have access to our historical documents?

6. Do we have a system of backing up our files?

7. Are the files and materials we record stored safely?

8. Do we actually use these files in our meetings or leadership training?

9. How organized and easy to search our the files we keep?

OUTREACH: A measurement of how well our organization communicates with other organizations and people

1. Do people in our community whom we serve, know we exist and what services we provide?

2. Are the fliers, articles, advertisements, social media posts, etc. we create to announce our events distributed at least two weeks prior to the event?

3. Do we set clear goals for attendance at our meetings and events?

4. Do we have a standard for determining what makes an event "well" or poorly attended?

5. Do the same people attend our meetings or events, or do we notice a significant number of new faces?

6. Do we rely only on the officers of our organization to do outreach, or do we involve lay members in this process as well?

7. Do we do outreach in our larger community to develop relationships with like-minded groups and people?

GENERAL BODY MEETINGS

1. Do our meetings occur in the same place, time and location, or do these variables change often?

2. Do our meetings start and end when they are supposed to?

3. Are the meetings we convene fun, informative and inspiring?

4. Do we disseminate or post written agendas for each meeting to our members? Do we follow the agenda, or do our meetings often steer off into other matters?

5. Are members given time to voice their opinions or ideas?

6. Is there always a secretary present to record minutes of our meetings?

7. Are meeting minutes posted online, in our office or in a newsletter for members who missed meetings?

8. Do we use our meetings to resolve issues, raise issues, debate ideas, and solicit assistance?

9. If we decide on doing something as an organization, do we set a specific timetable for when tasks should be completed? Do we determine specific people responsible for completing tasks?

10. Can members critique decisions or actions of the organization without being ostracized?

11. Are criticisms or ideas from members actually considered and/or implemented by the leadership?

12. Do leaders debrief after general body meetings?

CHARACTER/PERSONAL INTEGRITY

1. Do organization leaders do what they say, when they say they will?

2. Do leaders submit paperwork or complete important tasks in a timely manner?

3. When leaders communicate with outside people, do they promptly follow-up with those people via phone or email?

4. Are leaders accessible by members (office hours, phone, email, social media)?

5. Do leaders respond to phone calls or emails within one to two business days?

PROGRAMMING

1. Does our organization do events that inform and inspire members?

2. Does our programming reflect the vision and mission of our organization?

3. Do our events duplicate those of other organizations?

4. Do we use our events to promote our organization, recruit new members and solicit assistance?

5. Do our events draw good attendance?

6. Does our programming meet the needs of our membership?

7. Do we use our resources (financial and otherwise) to protect and advocate for the vulnerable and voiceless members of our larger community?

MORALE: A measurement of how well we inspire pride and positive feelings about our organization from its members.

1. Does our organization do a good job of promoting the benefits of joining our group?

2. Do we use promotional materials to instill a sense of pride and belonging (t-shirts, buttons, bumper stickers)?

3. Does the leadership officially recognize and publicly celebrate the achievements and contributions of individual members?

4. Do we create events that provide opportunities for our members to meet, encourage, and fellowship with each other?

These are just a few categories we need to consider in evaluating our organizations. Hopefully you find this information helpful. Our organizations must strive for excellence and effectiveness because so many people depend on them.

Conclusion

I've tried my best to include all of the basic information needed for you to run your Black Student Union in an effective and successful manner.

This little book has taken you through tactics, strategy, and the thinking of an effective leader and organization. I've shared years of my personal experiences and study of student activism. We've explored the history and purpose of a Black Student Union.

So you have an incredible resource in this handbook. But it means nothing if you don't discuss, implement and apply this information. Nor can you simply follow this book step-by-step and expect to be successful. While implementing the ideas in this handbook can put your organization way ahead of the leadership curve, you as a leader must always apply things to your own situation and set of circumstances, utilizing your knowledge of your particular campus dynamics and resources.

I spent much time and thought putting this handbook together. My hope is that you will continue the tradition of activism and service established by your predecessors. As I mentioned before, Black Student Unions exist on college campuses to promote Black solidarity, social justice and advocacy for Black students attending universities that are not always welcoming and supportive of our people. It is your job to provide the support and resources our people need to excel academically and the consciousness and activism they need to develop into strong and committed Black leaders and problem-solvers upon their graduation. I can teach you everything I know about leadership and activism, but I cannot teach you heart, motivation or a burning desire for excellence. These you must develop for yourself.

Perhaps I am too idealistic for my own good. But whatever the case, I expect this book to find its way into the hands of Black students, Black organizations (especially BSUs) on every college campus in America. I believe this handbook contains vital information and perspectives our college and community organizations need to be stronger, more organized and more effective. Unlike a speaker who comes and goes, this book is a resource you can reference as many times as you need to. So I humbly ask you to spread the word about the BSU Handbook. And hopefully I'll get the opportunity to meet you personally when I visit your campus to speak. If you are interested in reading my blog, please visit mytruesense.org. Likewise, if you'd like to learn more about me, my background, and activities, visit my website: http://truself143.wix.com/agyeityehimba

Agyei Tyehimba
October 26, 2014

ABOUT THE AUTHOR

Agyei Tyehimba is an educator, writer, and activist from Harlem, New York. He is the co-founder of KAPPA Middle School in the Bronx, New York. He has over 20 years experience as a schoolteacher, educator and youth development specialist.

Agyei co-wrote the Essence Bestselling memoir "Game Over: The Rise and Transformation of a Harlem Hustler," which was published by Simon & Schuster in 2007. In 2014, he wrote "Truth for our Youth: A Self-Empowerment Book for Teens."

A powerful speaker, Mr. Tyehimba has been featured on NY1 News, Huffington Post Live, C-Span and has appeared in the A&E documentary "The Mayor of Harlem: Alberto 'Alpo' Martinez."

Agyei is a professional consultant providing political advice and direction for Black student organizations, community activist groups, and nonprofits. Agyei earned his Bachelor's degree in sociology from Syracuse University, his Master's degree of Professional Studies in Africana Studies from Cornell University, and his Master of Arts degree in African American Studies from the University of Massachusetts at Amherst. You can read Agyei's blog of social and political commentary at mytruesense.org

Made in the USA
Middletown, DE
30 May 2018